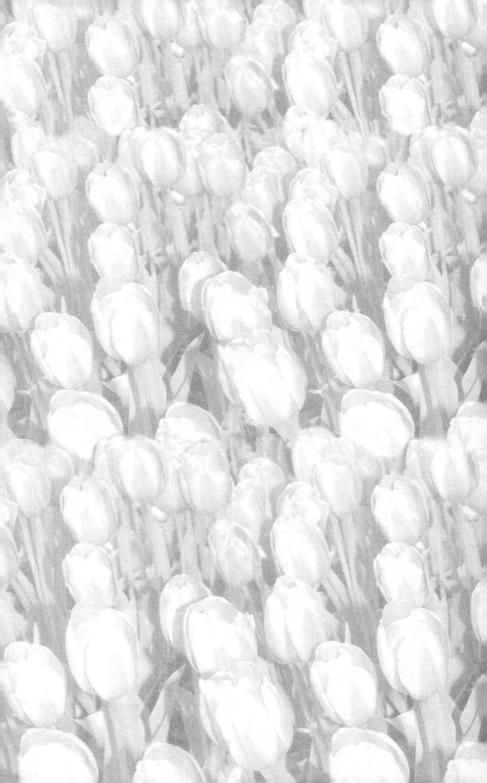

Canine Parables

Canine Parables

Portraits of God and Life

Paulette Zubel

MAGNUS PRESS

MAGNUS PRESS
P. O. Box 2666
Carlsbad, CA 92018

Canine Parables:
Portraits of God and Life

First edition, 1999

Printed in the United States of America

Copyedited by Janet Squires
Cover photo by Yvonne Swartz
LCCN: 99-74268

ISBN: 0-9654806-4-X

Publisher's Cataloguing-in-Publication
(Provided by Quality Books, Inc.)

Zubel, Paulette.
    Canine parables: portraits of God and life/
Paulette Zubel. — 1st ed.
      p. cm.
      LCCN: 99-74268
      ISBN: 0-9654806-4-X

      1. Christian life—Anecdotes. 2. God—Worship and love—Anecdotes. 3. Dogs—Behavior—Anecdotes. I. Title

BV4515.2.Z83 1999   231.7
                                   QB199-899

04 03 02 01 00 99   10 9 8 7 6 5 4 3 2 1

To the Father

and to my mother,

Justine Victoria Cramer

Special thanks to

Thomas Frank Zubel,

who kept me on track and to

Diana Wallis,

who kept me honest.

• C O N T E N T S •

GROWING IN GOD
FROM LIFE'S EXPERIENCES

A parable is a story which reminds us of something else,
and that something else is always the more important of the two.
—Robert Frost

Is a golden retriever a proper medium for addressing spirituality? In his parables, Jesus used ordinary images that were familiar to his listeners to teach about godliness, and he did not consider animals (e.g., sheep, birds, camels) to be unworthy teaching tools. Today, whether dog owners or not, most of us will have some contact with them. Thus, *Canine Parables* offers some spiritual insights that have come to mind while observing dogs.

This book is a collection of anecdotes that relate the naughty and eccentric as well as the adorable behaviors of canines. Matthew Henry wrote, "Even those creatures that are not dignified with the powers of reason are summoned in this concert (of praise), because God may be glorified in them."

Although each narrative begins with a quote given from a dog's point of view, the dogs have not been anthropomorphized, that is, given human characteristics; dogs are not people who happen to wear fur coats, and neither are they capable of making moral decisions. Dogs do, however, feel a range of emotions, and sometimes their facial expressions and body language speak volumes. And if you have pets, you probably will attest to their ability to communicate what they feel. Perhaps you, too, find it's fun to imagine what they might say if they could talk.

When I'm watching my dogs, God is not offended if at the same time my thoughts are upon him. So I'm giving the old saying—a dog is man's best friend—a new twist. These canine parables show that, with their wacky and winsome antics, our dogs can remind us that *God* is our best friend.

I won't be satisfied until my head is on the pillow.
                                        ~Lady the dog

Winston Churchill once commented, "I always manage somehow to adjust to any new level of luxury without whimper or complaint. It is one of my more winning traits." Churchill would have made a splendid dog. No creature adjusts to luxury as quickly as a dog.

When I was about five years old, my parents brought home a puppy—a strawberry-blond cocker spaniel. My mother named her Lady, "Because," Mom said, "she sat in the car like a little lady all the way home."

Over the next few months it became apparent that Lady's bloodline was questionable. As she got older her coat became redder, her nose sharper, and her legs long and thin. By the time she was fully grown she resembled a small Irish setter.

Though her pedigree was less than royal, this dog, like any true lady, soon learned to enjoy the niceties of life. She dined on fresh ground beef when she was pregnant, sprawled in front of the fire in winter, and got dibs on the window in the car.

When Lady placed one paw on the foot of the bed, however, Dad laid down the law: "She is *not* going to sleep on the bed." For several nights he and Lady engaged in a lot of paw pushing. Then one night Dad rolled over and there was Lady, staring him in the face. She was sitting on the floor, one paw and her chin resting on the bed next to his pillow. Dad laughed and Lady stared.

"Okay," Dad said, "you can get up here for just a few minutes—but you'd better stay down there by my feet!" Lady curled up on the foot of the bed, but by morning she was stretched out between my parents with her head on the pillow.

Many years later, a series of experiences reminded me of the way Lady finagled her way onto my parent's bed. I'd drifted away from God and in fact wrestled with the notion that God may not even exist. Then in a book I happened to have in my possession I read four powerful words: "Faith is a decision." I realized then that belief doesn't descend like a cloud from above; God allows people to make their own choices. When I recommitted my life to the Lord, no heavenly light descended over me, though I did feel a sense of relief and satisfaction.

But God was not quite satisfied. It was as if he had one paw on the bed and was determined to get closer. Soon I felt an urge to make a decision about Jesus. After reading and thinking, I concluded, *I can't reject the evidence that Jesus was God incarnate, that he died as a sacrifice for me, and was resurrected.*

It seemed God had his chin on the bed and was ready to make his leap. I felt a desire to know God more intimately, and the best way to do that is to read the Bible. So I began with Genesis, *Just one chapter a day*, I thought, *and—I suppose I could pray every day, too.* God knew I didn't have much experience praying; I'd always depended on myself to get things done. So I did what Jesus said to do: recite the Lord's Prayer.

By this time God seemed to be curled up on the mattress and eying the pillow. It wasn't long before I was observing a Sabbath, and by the time I'd read well into the New

Testament, my prayers had become more personal. I admitted to God that—sometimes—I could use a little guidance. I noticed changes in myself—a willingness to overlook small annoyances, to be less selfish, to ask my husband for advice. In a way that I can't explain, what began as a simple assent to believe led to acting in ways consistent with that belief.

God gives us free will, and no one forced me to let him into my life, any more than my dad was forced to let Lady onto the bed. He could have been hard nosed and made her stay on the floor. But Lady wanted up on the bed not just for the sake of comfort; she wanted to be near the people she loved, and I think Dad knew that. When one of his buddies got a new puppy, Dad laughed and said, "Don't let that little dog put even one paw on the bed. Next thing you know she'll be snoring on your pillow."

I was once determined that God wouldn't get even one paw on the bed. I could have hardened my heart and refused to let him near, but I knew he wanted to get close because he cares for me. I've got to admit I enjoy his company, so I guess I'm just going to have to get used to sharing my pillow.

> *Love bade me welcome; yet my soul drew back . . .*
> *[so] Love drew nearer to me.*
> *-George Herbert*

Never hide your chocolates in a bottom drawer.
~Perry the dog

The little cocker spaniel mix was the runt of Lady's last litter, and he was one laid-back puppy. All the prospective takers overlooked him when they chose their pets, but Perry seemed unconcerned. He napped in a corner of the basket and opened one eye when a littermate left in the arms of its new owner. He must have thought, *I'm not worried. The people who live here are a bunch of softies. They'll just keep me if no one else wants me.* That's exactly what happened, and our runt kept his easygoing personality even into adulthood.

In fact, that's how he came by his name. In the 1950s Perry Como, a popular singer, had his own TV show. Como was a very casual entertainer and either ambled around the stage or lounged on a stool during his act. Dad said, "That guy's real relaxed, just like our puppy." So we named the puppy Perry.

Perry was not the smartest dog in the world. Lady used to lure him away from the prime spot in front of the fireplace by running into another room and barking out the window. When Perry ran to see what Lady was barking at, she'd dash back and plop down in the coveted spot. It worked every time.

Though Perry was not a mental giant, there was nothing wrong with his sense of smell—as my mom discovered.

Mother invented the word "chocoholic," and since my sister and I also loved the stuff, my dad considered this fondness a female weakness. Mom tried not to give in to her "weakness," but every now and then she'd buy a box of chocolates. We three would each have some, then Mom would hide the rest so Dad wouldn't find out.

Once, she hid her stash in the bottom drawer of a dresser, between several layers of her underwear. Mother forgot, however, that we had a detective with a very sensitive nose.

Perry was built low to the ground, and it didn't take him long to catch a whiff of the secret stash. "What's the matter with that dog?" Dad said. He pointed to Perry, who was sitting in front of Mom's underwear drawer. "He's been staring at that same spot for fifteen minutes." Mom made big eyes and lifted her shoulders.

My mother is hardly the first person who tried to hide something. The book of Genesis tells us that Cain killed Abel in the Garden of Eden, then acted like nothing had happened. When God said, "Where's your brother?" Cain said, "How should I know?" Next thing you know, Cain was banished to the land of Nod.

Such direct administration of justice doesn't happen much these days. Within our criminal justice system the wrath of God seems to have been replaced by bureaucracy. The crime itself often gets buried between layers of hearings and plea bargains, and victims wonder if true justice is a reality.

Most of us will never become crime victims, but we all encounter our share of unfairness—from a critical boss or a pushy neighbor. Many people use the lack of divine intervention as an excuse for doubting the existence of God: "I can't believe there really is a God," they say. "Look at all the injustice in the world!" But the hope of ultimate justice seems a pretty good reason for believing there is indeed a just and trustworthy God.

I'll leave it to the theologians to argue the eternal consequences of hiding candy from one's husband. And I'll trust
the One whose senses go beyond sight and sound and smell,
who has a way of digging down into the bottom drawers and
discovering the things hidden there.   It's certain he'll find a
lot more than a box of chocolates. And it is certain, too, that
God would rather forgive than judge.

He is patient with you, not wanting anyone to perish,
but everyone to come to repentance.
–2 Peter 3:9

I'm smart, but I do some dumb things.
~ Lady the dog

Lady used to bark at her own reflection in the window. You might think that's pretty dumb, but dog trainers don't agree. A smart dog becomes easily bored and notices things that other members of the pack ignore—like her own reflection in glass.

Having a canine whiz kid has its pluses and minuses. On the plus side, Lady was entertaining. Besides yapping at her own reflection, she learned tricks and commands quickly. You already know how she lured Perry away from the fireplace.

She also practiced one-upmanship. Most dogs resist the "down" command; lying down is the ultimate expression of submission. We trained our dogs by using treats as a reward, so if Perry was given the "sit" command, Lady would dash in front of him and plop down on her stomach. Her trick was one better and clearly more deserving of the tidbit.

On the minus side, Lady was always looking for something to do. She never sat still and she grabbed anything that wasn't nailed down. Lady had her own chew toys, but they were BORRRING. Part of the fun was getting away with the booty.

Lady knew what "leave" meant: keep your mouth off. If Lady was carrying Dad's shoe, she'd obey the "leave" command, but then she'd grab my stuffed rabbit. I'd say "leave" and she'd grab my sister's souvenir pillow. It went on for months. Grab-the-slipper. Leave! Grab-the-towel. LEAVE! Grab-the-underwear. LEAVE!! A smart dog can be a real challenge.

But for such a smart dog, Lady sometimes sure acted dumb. I used to take her for walks on a leash and she'd stop to sniff at a signpost. Then instead of passing on in front of the post, she'd amble around behind it. When she got to the end of the leash, she'd circled around the post again. By this time there'd be about two inches of leash stretched between the post and her collar.

Then Lady would look at me and whine as if she had no idea that her legs could actually move in reverse. Her brains seemed to have drained out onto the grass, and she apparently expected to die there, trapped like . . . well, a dog.

I can think of some smart people in the Bible who did pretty dumb things. The book of Ruth, for instance, is also about the triumph of her mother-in-law, Naomi. You'd never guess it, though, by listening to Naomi.

She felt sorry for herself and made some foolish statements: "God has been mean to me. He took my husband and my two sons, and now I'm a widow—too old to have more children. I'm no use to anyone." But her daughter-in-law Ruth said, "No matter what, I'm going to stick by you."

They had no means of support, but Naomi was both shrewd and wise. She not only figured out a way for the two of them to survive, she guided Ruth into the arms of a kind and wealthy new husband.

Dogs and Bible figures do not hold the monopoly on being smart but acting dumb. I got high marks in high school and college, but I've made plenty of foolish decisions that, frankly, I don't care to talk about. To give you some idea, though—Dr. Laura Schlesinger wrote a book called

Ten Stupid Things Women Do to Mess Up Their Lives. I've done almost all of them.

That's why stories in the Bible about smart people acting dumb are among my favorites. It comforts me to know that wisdom coupled with foolishness is a characteristic shared by people who are beloved of God.

> *[We] should never be ashamed to own [we have]*
> *been foolish, which is but saying that [we are]*
> *wiser today than yesterday.*
> *—Jonathan Swift*

My mouth can be terrible or tender.
—Perry the dog

What Perry lacked in canine intelligence he made up for in looks. My parents had mated Lady with a pedigreed cocker spaniel, and most of her pups looked a lot like their sire. At maturity, Perry weighed about twenty pounds, and his moist eyes looked like coals against his platinum fur.

Like most dogs, Perry liked to carry things around, but we didn't realize what a tender mouth he had until the day of the tomato. I was about ten years old, and Dad and I were weeding in the garden. Perry was with us, snuffling around the plants, when dainty as you please he plucked a ripe tomato right off the vine.

A dog's natural instinct is to retrieve, so Perry took his prize to my father. Dad turned the tomato this way and that, then he grinned and said, "I'm glad you're here to see this; no one would believe me without a witness." Dad held out the tomato to me. "Perry sure has a delicate bite," he said. "He didn't put one tooth mark on this tomato." While Dad still held the tomato, Perry took it back and ate it.

Dad told the tomato story to all his friends, and they couldn't believe that a dog would eat vegetables. But my father was amazed that a dog's mouth—which could easily tear apart a chunk of raw meat—could be tender enough to pick a ripe tomato without damaging it.

It's not much of a leap to compare Perry's mouth to a verse from the book of James: "Out of the same mouth come praise and cursing" (3:10). Praise is tender to the ear while cursing tears at the soul. And words carry impact whether said aloud or uttered in the heart: thinking in destructive ways affects our attitudes.

I'm a writing tutor at a local community college. Todd asked me to look at a poem he'd written and tell him if it met his instructor's criteria. Because of Todd's slow speech and awkward mannerisms I suspected he had a learning disability. Sure enough, he was taking developmental English.

I gave him an indulgent smile and thought, *This is probably going to be the worst poem ever written.* In simple words and phrases, this young man had written about the frustrations and barriers he faced every day. The poem was so beautiful and poignant, I could literally feel my jaw drop.

"You know what?" I said. "This poem is so good, I wish I'd written it. Don't change a single word."

Todd beamed while he took several minutes to pack up his papers and books. And I mentally slapped my own wrists. What if my words had reflected what was originally in my heart? Todd's past was full of failures, his self-confidence as easily bruised as the skin of a ripe tomato. It was only by the grace of God that I held my tongue. What might have been a curse to Todd's spirit was replaced with praise.

Perry didn't always use discretion when he used his mouth. Tomatoes may have been safe from harm, but he once was none too gentle with my sister's diary. Though I show better judgment than Perry when I use my mouth, that's not to say I haven't caused my share of bruises. And though I'm learning which situations require tough words and which tender, I'm afraid I've left behind an occasional mangled tomato.

A wise man's heart guides his mouth.
–Proverbs 16:23

I don't like basements, but I do love you.
–Jet the dog

Hello. My name is Paulette, and I'm a recovering irresponsible pet owner. Here's my story. I'd had a succession of failed attempts at dog ownership and was ready to give up on the idea. But the rental community I'd just moved into allowed pets, so I gave it one more try.

Jet was supposed to be a cockapoo, but the breeder's guard must have been down when Jet's mother came in heat. As Jet matured, it was obvious something else had entered into the mix. He filled out into a low and stocky thirty pounder with pale shaggy fur and deep black eyes.

I'm not proud of the way I raised Jet. He was not neutered, didn't have a safe place to exercise, and on top of all that, he stayed in the basement all day while I worked. Still, his happy little tap dance of toenails on the tile floor greeted me when I came home each day after work.

Then when Jet was about four years old I met and married my husband, Tom, and life improved substantially for both Jet and me. The three of us moved into a rented house in a subdivision outside the city. I worked at home and Jet no longer had to stay in the cellar during the day. But for the rest of his life, Jet hated to go into basements.

The first time I went to the basement to do the laundry in our new place, Jet halted at the top of the stairs. He dropped to his belly, laid his head on his front paws, and peered down at me. When I called him, he wagged his little stub of a tail and raised himself to a sitting position, kneaded the floor with his front paws, then plopped back down on his belly. The conflict in his body language said it all: he wanted to be where I was, but the negative associations of his long, lonely days in a basement kept him pinned to the top step.

You can be sure I felt plenty guilty; I knew why he couldn't bring himself to come down those stairs. He didn't have the reasoning power to blame me for his bad feelings for the basement, but that didn't make me feel any better. And even though I'd cooped him up and neglected him, Jet was still devoted to me. In effect, he said "I hate the basement, but I love you."

It's not difficult to make the leap from Jet's perspective to the way God perceives sin and the sinner. When I turn green over my friend's new job, God is offended. But when I recognize my error, acknowledge it, and ask for forgiveness, God, like Jet, no longer associates me with the offense. In effect, God says, "I hate your sin, but I love you."

When Jet was no longer confined to the basement, he napped in sunny spots on the carpet, barked out the window at squirrels, and followed me from room to room while I dusted or straightened. He reveled in his freedom and in my company. Obviously, all was forgiven.

But when God forgives and forgets, *I'm* the one who's been brought up the basement steps: one step for lying to the telephone solicitor; another step for yelling at my husband; another for the catty remark about the aerobics instructor's red hair; every meanness, every deceit, every destructive impulse drops away and disappears below me. God leads me up from the darkness, and into a sunny room where the corners have been dusted and the clutter removed.

It's a dog's nature to let bygones be bygones, and it's God's nature to separate me from my offenses. But while Jet is careful to avoid the basement, I'm not as quick on the uptake. Once he got out of the basement, I couldn't drag Jet down there with a tractor. But God has to pull me back up the cellar stairs every day, because just as I'm still becoming a responsible pet owner, I'm still learning how to be a devoted Christian.

As far as the east is from the west,
so far has he removed our transgressions from us.
~Psalm 103:12

If you sound mad, I won't come.
—Jet the dog

"Whuff!" Jet barked at a squirrel.

"Jet!" I snapped. "Be quiet!"

"Whuff!" He always had to have the last word.

Then I looked down for only a minute, and when I looked up, he was in the middle of the road. I was angry that my dog had slipped away from me, and I was worried that he might get hit by a car. So I screwed up my face and screeched at him. "Jet! You get over here right now!"

He didn't budge. Obviously I needed a different strategy. I faked a cheerful voice and clapped my hands, and he came right to me. I praised him—then vowed to watch him closer when we were outside.

Jet didn't want to come the first time I called because he knew by my body language and tone of voice that I was angry. He'd seen me that way before, and on the first occasion he didn't know what to expect. His dark eyes shone as he galloped up to me, but I rewarded him with a scolding. Then I marched him into the house. After that, when Jet knew I was mad he wasn't anxious to come to me. I don't blame him. Would you be eager to approach someone if you knew the consequences could be unpleasant?

That particular experience with Jet reminds me of my first encounter with evangelism. When I was about thirteen, my friend Rebecca invited me to her church. The preacher talked about sin and wickedness and the agonies of hell.

That sermon took place over three decades ago in a small rural community, long before drugs and easy sex. The wickedest thing I'd ever done was pocket some doll clothes from a five and dime when I was eight years old. I wondered, *Would God send a thirteen-year-old to hell for once stealing a doll dress? If so, He must be a very angry God.*

But the preacher said that all my burdens would be lifted by trusting Christ as Savior. I didn't fully understand what "trusting Christ" meant, but I dreaded the consequences if I didn't.

A couple of years later I left that church, and over the ensuing years I spent a lot of energy avoiding my responsibilities to God. While I never stopped believing, I was afraid to draw near to God because I knew he'd be angry with me. I was a lot like Jet, standing in the middle of the road, afraid to come, and at the same time afraid to run away. Jet didn't understand my concern for his well-being, and likewise, I didn't understand how God cared for me; I believed in him because I was afraid not to.

But God never stopped believing in me. When my mother was dying from lung cancer and I was in a position of need, God gave me the opportunity to read some Christian books. They explained about sin, and separation from God, and how God's love redeems us.

At last I understood that God is not all wrath and judgment, that his anger is directed at sin, not the sinner. And it isn't sin alone that condemns us. If that were true, no one would get to heaven. Separation from God occurs because we reject God, not because he rejects us.

In all fairness, if at thirteen I'd been able to articulate my fears, someone at that little church in my hometown probably could have set me straight. But all I heard from the pulpit was God's anger and condemnation. This was supposed to win souls.

And it worked—just like it worked the first time Jet responded to me when I was angry. But after that first time, Jet kept his distance when he knew I was mad, and after my first approach to God, I kept my distance from him because I remembered all the talk about his wrath.

I learned that Jet was a lot more willing to get close to me when I smiled and opened my arms to him. And when I understood that God waits with open arms, that he is the loving and forgiving Master, I began to close the distance between us.

You are a gracious and compassionate God,
slow to anger and abounding in love.
—Jonah 4:2

Sitting by the fire is more fun than vacuuming the floor.
-Jet the dog

Jet hated the vacuum cleaner. I'm not fond of it myself, but sweeping the carpet is a necessary evil. Jet seemed to think the machine itself was quite evil indeed, a noisy beast that attached itself to my arm and threatened our well-being. Come to think of it, he may have had a point.

Whenever I used the vacuum Jet would either (1) bark at it and snap at the little plastic wheels or (2) hide under the bed. If I could have squeezed under there, I might have joined him.

Jet did like some human contraptions, though. At the first turn of the can opener or hum of the microwave oven, he was immediately under foot. But his favorite human contrivance was the fireplace. He was definitely an indoor dog with fine hair and cold blood. The first house Tom and I bought had a fireplace, and the hearth rug became one of Jet's favorite spots. He'd cozy up to the heat until his fur got so hot he'd have to back off.

Sometimes when we had a fire, I'd sit on the floor in front of the sofa. Dogs, being pack animals, like to make body contact with other pack members, that being my husband and me. So when I got on the floor, he'd cuddle up close and pant in my face—Jet that is, not my husband. This, I'm sure, was his idea of doggie heaven.

One evening I said to Jet, "Oh, sure, when we're by the fire you want to be my pal. But when I'm vacuuming? Nooooo. That's work! Then it's 'Adios, amigo—I'm outta here.'"

That statement to my dog reflects the attitude of some of us humans who call ourselves Christians. I'm eager to accept God's blessings, but sometimes I'm not as willing to fulfill my responsibilities.

God has granted me many blessings—a nice husband, a car that runs, an affinity for the written word. I benefit also from blessings that are not mine alone—black-eyed Susans, a fresh breeze on a sultry afternoon, scarlet maples against a cobalt sky. All these gifts, like a fire on a winter evening, warm the soul.

But when it's time to give back to God, to share in the work of being a Christian, I'm less diligent about keeping my end of the bargain. Sometimes I'm too tired at night to read a chapter from the Bible, and sometimes my mind wanders when I'm praying. I'm not always as patient or as generous as God would like me to be.

And in the same way that Jet feared and misunderstood the vacuum cleaner, I fear and do not understand many of life's dark beasts. For two summers I worked at a camp for children with cystic fibrosis (CF). That's a terminal disease that creates thick mucus in the lungs and causes a chronic cough.

Have you ever had a nagging cough that hangs on for days? I have and it's tiring. My back aches, my stomach aches, and my chest aches from all the hacking. Children with CF are harassed by coughing twenty-four hours a day, every single day they live. The unrelenting hacking leaves them thin, pale, and exhausted. I admit I'll never understand why these children must suffer so and then die young. To say, "It's a mystery of God," just doesn't cut it.

But sticking with God even when I don't like or understand what's happening is a responsibility of being a

Christian. God, though, doesn't expect me to like everything; he doesn't expect me to understand everything. But because I've made the choice to join his pack, he does expect me to trust the pack leader.

When Jet attacked the vacuum or hid from it, I didn't feel insulted or abandoned. I knew he was merely expressing his displeasure while I performed a necessary chore. In the same way, God is tolerant when I bark at life's dragons or when I'm tempted to hide from them. He can handle my fears and my anger, and at the same time accomplish his plans. And when life blows in the occasional blizzard, I am comforted in knowing that, even though I have not always hauled in my share of the wood, I can trust God to keep a fire going in the grate.

We are prepared and eager to work with Christ through the sunny days in Galilee, but are we facing with Him the dark mysteries of life?
–Arthur John Gossip

Pulling on the leash is hard on my neck.
—Jet the dog

The lady walking in front of Jet and me glanced over her shoulder.

"Don't worry," I said, "there isn't a steam engine behind you. It's just my dog."

Jet liked to be in the lead on our walks—HAAAGH-HAAAGH-HAAAGH—and pulled hard on the leash. He always wanted to lead the way—HAAAGH-HAAAGH-HAAAGH—but would be jerked up short if I turned a corner or stopped to look at something. After a couple of miles, though, Jet got tired, then he'd slow down and walk beside me.

I don't know why that dog never put two and two together: "Hmm . . . when I pull on the leash my neck hurts and I choke; when I walk by Paulette my neck feels better and I can breath." He never got the message.

Still, I can identify with Jet's eagerness to set the course. I sometimes charge ahead and try to make things happen my way. Then I become weary at heart when God doesn't take me where I expected to go.

After I graduated from college, a series of fortunate events led to some freelance projects for a major Christian publisher. I noticed an interesting coincidence; I'd often be proofreading just the right book at the right time. When my mother was dying, I was assigned a book that addressed death and dying, heaven and angels. The book was such a comfort to me that I was sure it had been God's purpose all along to connect me with that publishing company.

Then out of the blue I was offered an in-house position. I didn't pray about it, nor did I ask for advice; I charged ahead, sure that God had engineered this unique opportunity. Within a few months I knew I'd made a mistake. A regular desk job in a bustling industry was not what I needed at this point in my life. This time I prayed and talked it over with my husband. Soon I was back to freelancing and I felt like I was doing what I was meant to do.

Like Jet and me, Jacob in the Old Testament was also determined to take the lead. As the second son, he was not entitled to the larger portion of his father's estate, nor to his father's special blessing. But through trickery and deceit Jacob took both the blessing and the bigger inheritance.

Still, God had big plans for Jacob, but this headstrong young man had to first learn to take direction. Jacob, though, did not accept direction willingly, so for one whole night he and God wrestled for control. Jacob at last yielded and later received a tremendous blessing: he fathered twelve sons, and those sons became the patriarchs of twelve tribes, from which sprang the nation of Israel.

Sometimes maturity reveals that there is wisdom in following. As Jet got older he became more willing to walk by my side rather than charge ahead. Jacob and I also yielded the lead because we matured, but our maturity was spiritual rather than physical.

That's not to say neither of us ever struggled again. Humans have a hard time yielding control to God one hundred percent of the time. So, I pray not only for God's will to be done in my life but, because Jacob did not hold a monopoly on wanting one's own way, I also pray for help in yielding to that will. Sure, I like having my own way, but I'd prefer not to spend a whole night wrestling with God.

There are two kinds of people: those who say to God,
"Thy will be done," and those to whom God says,
"All right, then, have it your way."
–C.S. Lewis

They call me Mister dog.
~George the dog

A Haitian proverb says, "A dog is just a dog unless he's facing you—then he's *Mister* Dog." I'd never appreciated that proverb until my encounter with George.

After Tom and I moved into our house, we had a couple of visitors: a big, red Chesapeake Bay retriever and a long-haired, black mutt. These two guys wandered the neighborhood almost daily, and I called them Lenny and George, from John Steinbeck's *Of Mice and Men*. Big red looked like a George to me.

Like a fool, I offered the dogs a hand-out, but I soon found out that George had a short memory when it came to appreciating the hand that handed-out.

Jet and I were out for a walk when we encountered George. He was standing in the middle of the road, barking at cars. When one of them tooted, George just stood there barking and the car had to drive around him.

When I spoke to George, his countenance did not encourage familiarity. I took a couple of steps toward him and he growled. Contrary to the old saying, a wagging tail does *not* always mean a dog is friendly. George wagged, but he did not appear at all friendly.

I crept backwards and pulled Jet along with me, although he didn't require much coaxing. When there was sufficient pavement between George and us, I turned and walked back home.

You can bet I never gave George or his pal Lenny any

more handouts. I didn't much like George after that, but I had more respect for him. He no longer seemed like the neighbor's harmless pet.

I used to regard troubles in the same way that I related to George. Misfortune visited me by way of the newspaper or TV, but I gave them little attention while they passed by. Then I became the target of a crime, and I no longer looked at trouble in the same way that I'd looked at George—transient, something that belonged to my neighbor.

When trouble violated my sense of security, I felt betrayed. Before, trouble had, like George, been only a benign visitor. But trouble growled at me and I quickly developed a lot more respect for it.

I'm not glad I encountered trouble, but I found that in the midst of distress God often delivers compensation. I could more easily empathize with other people who'd experienced life-changing trouble—the lady at aerobics who has a learning disabled child, the man at school whose granddaughter is addicted to drugs, the returning student who is going through a divorce. Before, when I encountered troubled people, I felt guilty (in comparison my life was trouble-free), or afraid (their trouble might rub off on me), or awkward (what should I say—or not say?).

Now I know that I don't need to say much—I only need to listen.

My trouble with George frightened me, and being frightened made me angry. So after that when George wandered into the yard I ran out and yelled, "You get outta here . . . Mr. Dog!" Trouble breeds respect. After my encounter with crime I was frightened and angry, too. Those feelings eventually went away, but the respect for trouble remains—I'm no longer fearful, but I *am* more cautious. So too remains my respect for those who have looked trouble in the mouth and have responded in admirable ways.

Like the woman whose husband divorced her for someone younger. When I said, "That must have been a blow to your self-esteem," she said, "At first. But when I returned to school I found out I'm good at being a student, and now whole new worlds are opening up."

I'm no Pollyanna. I get anxious when I think about the misfortunes I might encounter. But God has already helped me through a lot, and I can only pray that he will give me what I need the next time I meet Mr. Trouble.

He knows not his own strength
that hath not met adversity.
–Ben Jonson

It's hard to pick up a stick when I'm lying on it.
–Jet the dog

Do dogs get senile? As Jet got older he was sometimes forgetful. Once, he teased for five minutes straight to go out when I was up to my elbows in meatloaf. He dashed to the door and back and hopped from one leg to the next.

So I splashed some water over my hands and grabbed the doorknob. The water and grease made my hands slip off, so I leaped over the dog to get a paper towel. By this time Jet was grinding his teeth.

When I opened the kitchen door, Jet scrabbled across the porch tiles and hurled himself at the outside door. That door opens inward so he backpedaled while I opened it. Then he leaped over the bottom step, scurried onto the grass—and stopped to chew on the creeping Charlie. He completely forgot what he went outside to do.

Another time Jet and I were outside together. While I sweated at raking leaves, Jet lounged in the sun chewing on a stick between his front paws. The rest of the stick was tucked under his body. He must have forgotten that, though, because when I called him, he tried to pick up the stick before he stood up. It took him a couple of tries before he figured out what the deal was. I laughed and said, "It's hard to pick up a stick when you're lying on it."

That statement reminds me of what psychologists call "self-defeating behaviors" (SDBs)—things people do to guarantee their own failures—like when I buy a bag of Oreos the day after going on a diet.

But SDBs can prevent more than a change in silhouette. Take the Israelites, for instance. They were a people especially favored by God. God led them through the desert, fed them, and orchestrated their every success. At last they stood at the border of Canaan—the land God had promised them. The land was so fertile that grapes were the size of walnuts and cattle were so fat they could hardly walk. "This is some awesome place," said the Israelites, "but look at those Canaanites! We look like little bugs compared to them."

So the Israelites—defeated by their own fearful behavior—wandered in the desert for forty years.

I'm not immune to SDBs either. A few years ago my freelance business wasn't taking off. I became discouraged and took a part-time clerical job, then tried to justify my decision.

"There's nothing wrong with clerical work," I said to Tom.

"That's true," he said.

"Even though," I said, "it's the same kind of work I was doing twenty years ago."

"Well . . . yes."

"And it uses up time I could be using to promote my freelance business."

"Mm . . ." this was a grunt.

"You think I should quit, don't you?"

He opened his mouth, "Well—"

"Well, my freelance business wasn't going anywhere!"

Tom pursed his lips.

"And," I said, "I suppose you think that taking this job practically guarantees that it never will go anywhere."

Silence. I hate it when he's right.

Like Jet, I couldn't pick up the stick because I was lying

on it. Like the Israelites, I was afraid I wouldn't succeed, so I acted in a way that let me avoid trying. Self-defeating behavior.

A dog, of course, doesn't wrestle with an inferiority complex or struggle under a load of emotional baggage. Once Jet discovered the problem with the stick, he immediately overcame it. We who are the logical, analytical species, prefer to wander in the desert.

People wish to learn to swim
and at the same time keep one foot on the ground.
–Marcel Proust

Your tears rock my boat.
—Jet the dog

They'll never convince *me*. Some animal behaviorists claim that my dog isn't really comforting me when I weep, that he cuddles up when I'm crying and licks my tears because he likes salt water. Well, Jet may have liked salt, but he wagged his tail when he liked something, and he never wagged his stub when I cried. I'm not saying that Jet felt anything like compassion, but he was not indifferent to the emotions I showed in body language and tone of voice.

Jet would whine when he heard me crying, then he'd wiggle close, jerk his nose down and up a couple of times and wiggle closer. His eyes grew round and turned almost black, and the expression of concern on his face was so sincere I could almost hear him say, "Whaaat?" His obvious distress moved me and I produced a sound halfway between a gasp and a wail. At which Jet jabbed his nose in my face and his whole manner suggested anxiety. He didn't understand why the one he trusted and looked up to—the leader of his pack—was acting so weird.

Peter, the disciple of Jesus, must have felt a little like Jet at times. Like when Lazarus was sick. First, instead of rushing to help his friend, Jesus took no action for two days. I can imagine Peter thinking, *Jesus loves Lazarus and I've seen Jesus heal sick people with less effort than I use to blow my nose. Why does he delay?*

Then, Jesus at last arrives at the home of Lazarus but learns the man has died. At which news, Jesus wept. Jesus wept? How do you think Peter reacted to that? I'd guess that Peter—like Jet—felt insecure and anxious. Can you blame him? Jesus could have saved Lazarus but didn't, and now he was crying about it. Jesus had not acted at all the way Peter would expect.

Just as I was the primary resource from whom Jet received dog chow and companionship, Jesus had become Peter's primary resource—Jesus, who fed thousands with a few scraps of bread and fish, and who restored life to the dead. And now Jesus was weeping over death.

It's not hard to see why Peter would be bewildered. At times I've wondered just what God was up to. My friend Doris had for a long time been looking for work in her field, and she was growing discouraged and depressed. I prayed that something would turn up soon, and sure enough, I heard about an opening that was perfect for her. She sent her resume, got an interview, and ten days later got a letter: "Thank you for your interest but the job has been given to another applicant."

When I first saw that job posting I was certain that God was answering my prayers for Doris. I was confused and upset because God hadn't responded the way I expected him to. And, like Jet, all I could do was approach the One I trusted and depended on, look up and say, "Whaaat?"

Jet's anxiety, though, was always relieved. His leader eventually returned to her old self, washed her face, and fixed him a snack. Even Peter understood everything in the end. His leader died, but was resurrected. And he gave Peter a job so full of purpose that it consumed him for the rest of his life.

As for me, sometimes I'm *sure* I understand what God is doing, sometimes I *think* I understand, but most of the time

I haven't a clue. Doris is still struggling and I'm still praying for her. I'm also praying that God will help me to trust him and to not be anxious about the way he's behaving. And he has promised that one day everything will be clear, and I will know why at times my Leader seems to act so strange.

Now I know in part; [when perfection comes] I shall know fully.
-1 Corinthians 13:10, 12

Don't be afraid to say good-bye.
—Jet the dog

Grape Kool-Aid, sand, and the *Grapes of Wrath*—sounds like a nice way to spend a Sunday afternoon in August. Except I wasn't at the beach. I was sitting under the oak tree in the front yard and the sand was *in* the Kool-Aid. Jet had dug out a cool crater for his belly next to my lawn chair, and a goodly portion of the dirt landed in my drinking glass. He had a pretty strong kick for an old guy.

At the age of fifteen Jet was still reasonably spry. His hearing and eyesight were failing, but he could still run up and down steps and go for walks on the leash. He still barked at the vacuum cleaner and followed me around while I did chores.

Then one Sunday evening Jet had a seizure. On Monday morning Dr. Leali, the veterinarian, told me Jet had suffered a stroke. "Jet is in pain," said the doctor. "If he were my dog, I'd put him to sleep." We'd been taking Jet to Dr. Leali for ten years and I trusted his judgment.

I chose not to stay with Jet when the shot was administered because I knew I'd bawl my head off. My face twists up and gets ugly when I cry, and I didn't want to embarrass myself in front of the veterinarian. But in the weeks that followed Jet's death, I felt heavy at heart. My little friend had provided joy and companionship for fifteen years, but because of my vanity and self-consciousness I abandoned him in his last few moments of life.

Elisabeth Kubler-Ross identified the stages of grieving—

denial, anger, guilt, bargaining, acceptance. I went through them all-big time.

Denial: *I just can't believe he's gone.*

Guilt: *I wish Jet's earlier years had been more pleasant for him.*

Anger (at myself): *What a coward I am! I should have stayed with my poor little boy at the end.*

Acceptance: *Everything that lives must die, and Jet's last years were good ones. He was happy and healthy to the very end.*

The bargaining came last: *I'll make up for the mistakes I made with Jet.*

I meant that my next dog would benefit because of what I'd learned about caring for animals. But as it turned out, Jet's legacy had even greater importance.

My mother, a lifetime smoker, was diagnosed with terminal lung cancer. Mom was not afraid, but she wanted to handle the dying process in her own way—just pain management and maintaining her dignity. My father had died several years ago, so my sister and I took care of Mom in the small house that Dad had built with his own hands. It was Mother's wish to die in that house, and with the help of God and Hospice her wishes were honored.

During the last few hours of Mother's life, I remembered the lesson Jet's death had taught me. I'd never seen a person die before and I was afraid. But if I'd experienced regret over abandoning Jet, how much worse would I feel if fear kept me from my mother's side. In the end, there was nothing to fear. Mom died without pain or anxiety, in the presence of those who loved her.

I bawled my head off without caring one whit how ugly I looked. And I'll forever be thankful to God for using a dog to guide me down a more worthy path.

Do I believe dogs were created specifically as a teaching aid? No, but it's not hard to imagine God saying about a dog, "You'll receive a lot more than you can ever give." And who does that remind me of?

How powerfully God can speak to us all through
the ordinary . . . if we pay attention.
–Luci Shaw

Don't judge my quality by the appearance of my coat.
~Velvet the puppy

"I want a big black dog with big white teeth," I said.

At the time Jet died, Tom was away a lot on business. So I wanted not only a companion animal, but a dog who looked intimidating. Jet was the best dog in the world, but his button eyes and shaggy face didn't scare anybody.

Betsy, the attendant at the humane society, showed me a three-month-old Labrador retriever mix. "Here's a black puppy," she said, "and she'll probably get pretty big."

I crouched next to the cage and stuck two fingers through the wire. The puppy lay in the far corner and gazed at me. I said, "Hello," in that silly falsetto people use when talking to babies and small animals.

The puppy dipped her head and padded over to me. She wagged her tail but held it low. This puppy didn't look like she'd grow up to scare off an intruder. *Well,* I started making compromises in my mind, *she doesn't have to become a vicious watchdog. If she grows big enough, her size and her bark will intimidate anyone bent on mischief.* Still, I'd rather hoped for a puppy that was at least cute. But this pup's fur was dull and scruffy, and she was already into the gangly stage, with long skinny legs and a narrow muzzle.

Betsy opened the cage and when I picked up the puppy I could easily feel her ribs and spine. "She's awfully skinny," I said. The puppy then pressed her head into my neck, and the fur on her cheek felt as soft as velvet.

True to first indications, Velvet turned out to be a very sweet dog—as well as a protective one. She gives me sympathy when I cry, barks a warning when a stranger comes up the drive, and rarely strays far from my side. Velvet reminds me that a homely exterior can disguise a treasure of great worth.

The same could be said for some ordinary clay water-jars in the village of Cana. In the second chapter of his Gospel, the apostle John relates Jesus' first recorded miracle. He told the servants at a wedding party to fill some clay jars with water, but when the contents were poured into glasses, the water had become excellent wine.

For me, that first miracle—transforming the ordinary contents of homely vessels into something far better—represents the essence of Jesus' ministry on earth. His mission was to transform humankind, starting from the inside out. His concern lay with the human heart, and he wasn't put off by ugliness.

But within the suffering body and diseased soul, Jesus saw something else—a troubled heart, seeking rest. And that's what he most wanted to touch and to transform. Jesus restored deformed bodies, but his ministry had already sparked belief in many a sickened heart. Jesus said it himself: "Your faith has healed you."

The passing of centuries has not diminished the power of Jesus' touch. Just as the servants in Cana were well aware of what had been poured into the clay jars, so I am well aware of what I've poured into my heart, drop by drop—every lie, every petty thought, every selfish desire. My contents haven't changed as quickly as did the water at Cana; in the case of people, the transformation takes a little longer— a whole lifetime.

Like the jars at Cana, Velvet's unextraordinary exterior disguised something special. When she snuggled against me and expressed her need, her looks didn't matter to me any more.

Jesus, too, ignores outward appearance and looks straight to the heart. And when his transforming work is at last finished, the ordinary will become choice, because the heart of a seeker becomes special when touched by the hand of God.

*But we have this treasure in jars of clay
to show that this all-surpassing power is from God.
—2 Corinthians 4:7*

Grabbing the wallet and keys means bye-bye in the car.
~Velvet the puppy

"I'm afraid she's a little spoiled," I said.

Dr. Leali chuckled and gave Velvet her final puppy shot. "I can't imagine how that happened," he said. "She must have gotten out and one of the neighbors spoiled her."

Tom and I don't have children, and I'm home with Velvet during the day. So I talk to her while I fold the laundry, pet her while I watch the news, and give her treats for no particular reason.

Because we spend so much time together, Velvet quickly learned to read my body language, especially how I got ready to go someplace. When I pack my aerobics bag or my school bag, she shuffles behind me to the porch and settles on her pillow. But when I grab just my wallet and keys, her whole demeanor changes. She stands at attention with her ears forward, and her pupils become huge. Sometimes, you see, I take Velvet for a spin just because she enjoys a ride. (This is not, of course, the same as spoiling her.)

Velvet has learned to recognize signs—indications that have special meaning. Many biblical figures asked for and received signs. Gideon, for instance, left a piece of wool out overnight. "Lord," he said "if there's no dew on this wool in the morning, I'll know that you want me to lead Israel into battle."

One or two of my acquaintances say they've gotten this kind of dramatic indication, but I never have. The signs I get are not as readily identifiable as such—mostly because I recognize them after the fact. I ticked off a list to Steve, a skeptical acquaintance of mine.

• I quit a dead-end job and within a month my freelance business started to take off. I saw it as a sign I made the right decision. Steve said it was coincidence.

• I hadn't heard from a client for weeks. Then one afternoon I had a chance encounter with one of the client's employees, and on the way home I saw a rainbow. Two days later the client called and offered me a project. "Coincidence," says Steve.

• I missed an important appointment and when I called to apologize, she said, "Didn't you get my message? I couldn't make it." I say it's a sign God is involved in even my smallest concerns. "Another coincidence," said Steve.

I listed a few more examples, and Steve insisted that each instance was sheer happenstance. "What," I asked, "would you consider to be a sure sign from God?"

"I'm not sure," he said, "something like a miracle, I guess, but it would have to be a lot more convincing than a few examples of fortunate timing." Steve insisted that I looked at incidents in retrospect and translated plain good luck as a sign.

Truth is, it's occurred to me that my "signs" were an attempt to spiritualize dumb luck. Steve's countering every one of my examples with "coincidence," though, reminds me of the Pharisees of Jesus' day.

They knew of the ancient prophecies that described the Messiah, yet when Jesus stood before them, and said, "Look in the Scriptures; I'm the one the ancient prophecies speak about," they refused to acknowledge him.

"Like a lot of other phonies," they said, "you fulfill parts of the Scriptures, but that's just coincidence."

Steve said only something dramatic would make him believe in signs from God. But I wonder. The Pharisees witnessed Jesus healing the blind and deaf, but still he wasn't their idea of a Messiah. They wanted a mighty avenger from God who would restore Israel's former glory. Now *that* would be convincing.

Velvet knows that when I grab my keys and my wallet it often means she's going for a ride. She has enough sense to recognize signs. So too did some people in Jesus' day: the humble, the sick, the poor, the desperate—they recognized signs from God when they saw them.

Maybe Steve is right. Perhaps I see signs only because I want to see them. Or perhaps he doesn't see signs because, like the Pharisees, he doesn't want to. I guess some people just don't get it.

My eye shall never know the dry disease
Of thinking things no more than what it sees.
—Richard Wilbur

• FACING OUR DOUBTS •

When it thunders, I hide in the bathtub.
—Velvet the puppy

Right off I'll tell you that Velvet is not a 'fraidycat—uh—dog. Just because she's docile doesn't mean she's timid, but we all have something we're afraid of. In Velvet's case it's thunder. Whenever there's a storm, Velvet creeps under tables or hides behind furniture. Once I found her in the bathtub. Our bathroom is the darkest, quietest room in the house, and once when I snapped on the light during a storm, there she was, sitting in the skim of water that refuses to go down the drain.

Hiding is not necessarily a bad thing. Sometimes it's downright sensible, like during a tornado or being chased by a mob carrying sharp sticks. At other times the urge to hide is a reflex, and it is not limited to hiding oneself physically. I've felt like hiding from certain thoughts.

Before I recommitted to my faith, I was plagued by doubts: Does God really exist? Was Jesus really resurrected? Is there a conscious existence after death? I wanted to hide when my doubts and confusion popped up at unexpected moments—when I was alone in the car or just before I went to sleep.

But I knew that faith is a decision, and I said to myself, ***Regardless of my doubts, I want to believe and I'm going to believe.*** I felt like I'd come out of hiding, but my doubts and confusion didn't automatically go away; and because they still pestered me I felt deficient as a Christian.

Then I ran across a story in the New Testament—

Mark 9:17-29. A young boy was possessed by a demon that took away the boy's speech. Jesus' disciples couldn't help, so the boy's father approached Jesus, "Help us," he said, "if you can." "*If* I can?" said Jesus. "Don't you believe?" "I do believe," said the father. "Help me overcome my unbelief." Jesus drove out the demon and later told his disciples, "This kind can come out only by prayer."

When doubt and confusion bedeviled me, instead of confronting my feelings I hid from them. So, in effect, my doubts were like a demon that robbed me of speech, not because of unbelief but because I, like the boy's father in the story, needed help with my unbelief—and still need help every day for every doubtful thought.

How do I get help? It's in the story: Jesus said, "This kind can come out only by prayer." So I talk to God about my doubts: "Sometimes I don't understand what you're doing."

Our God is a God of truth. He knows that some things about Christianity are hard to believe, and he already knows what's in my heart. So if I haven't been struck by lightening for thinking, I certainly won't be struck down for praying.

While Velvet sometimes retreats to the bathroom during a storm, I no longer hide from confusion and doubt. I didn't say I no longer *have* confusion and doubt—I'm just no longer afraid of them.

Doubt is not the opposite of faith, but the central point . . . between faith (with all its demands) and unbelief (with all its consequences).
–Donald Bridge

I love you, but I don't like the fire.
~Velvet the puppy

Velvet is frustrated and I'm perplexed. This is not at all what I expected.

All dogs love to stretch out in front of a fire, and we were looking forward to Velvet's first reaction to the fireplace. She trotted back and forth beside Tom when he brought in the wood. And when he set down the kindling box she poked her head in and helped herself to a twig. But when the fire took off, Velvet licked the end of her nose a few times then slunk toward the far end of the room.

When I sat on the floor and called to her, she crept over to me with her head and tail low. She even sat next to me for a few seconds, but then she circled me and retreated. Velvet was clearly not enchanted with the fireplace.

In fact, she was downright frustrated. She made whistling noises from across the room and once or twice got close but changed her mind. So for the rest of the evening she stared and whistled. She wanted to get close to us but she didn't like where we were.

I felt that way about Sharon. I met Sharon in a literature class in college and we hit it off right away. We were the only students in class who remembered Howdy Doody and we both loved chocolate. Sharon always said nice things about her husband, so when she casually mentioned that she was having an affair I was stunned. I really liked Sharon and hoped we'd grow close, but she was sitting too close to a fire and I was uncomfortable near the heat.

So what did I do? I wimped out. I smiled and squirmed—then changed the subject. Sharon took my reaction as tacit approval and wanted to talk about Bob, her lover, every time we had coffee. I did so much squirming Sharon must have thought that I wore tight underwear.

I knew I wasn't handling the situation well. I wondered, *What would be the godly thing to do? What would Jesus say to Sharon?* It so happens I have a pretty good idea. John 8:1-11 tells about Jesus' encounter with a woman caught in the act of adultery. The religious experts wanted to stone her, but Jesus said to them, "He among you who is without sin cast the first stone." The accusers went away and Jesus said to the woman, "I do not condemn you. Go now, and leave your life of sin."

Without condoning the woman's adultery, Jesus gave her a chance to reexamine her behavior. What more could a friend do?

In the end I did what Velvet had done—I warily circled Sharon and told her how I felt. "Sharon," I said, "I like you, but to be honest I'm not comfortable when you talk about your affair. What you're doing could be very destructive." I hoped she'd take the message to heart.

"I know," she said, "but I'm just not ready to stop seeing Bob."

"If you decide to break it off with this guy," I said, "I'll support you any way I can—you can call me any time day or night. But if I act like your affair doesn't bother me, that would be sending you the wrong message."

After our chat, Sharon always seemed to have research to do and we stopped having coffee together. After the lit class ended I never saw her again.

Velvet sent Tom and me a clear message when we sat by

the fire. But just as Sharon wouldn't budge, Tom and I didn't move just to make Velvet feel better. The consequences for us were not serious—we just had to put up with Velvet's whistling. In Sharon's case, however, her whole family might have been destroyed.

Jesus didn't camp out by the woman's tent to make sure she reformed, so we don't know if she changed her way of life. The Bible shares truth, but it also leaves a lot unknown. So being a Christian doesn't mean I have all the answers. It does mean, though, that I might sometimes lose a potential friend.

If someone is caught in a sin, you who are spiritual should restore [her] gently. . . . In this way you will fulfill the law of Christ.
–Galatians 6:1–2

When it's urgent, I'll rub my whiskers in your face.
~Velvet the dog

Experts say that when dogs are content, they do nothing. Velvet, then, must be one contented dog. She spends hours without moving a muscle.

Even as a puppy she was not especially energetic. When she got her first collar she scratched at it a couple of times, then shrugged and took a nap. At the veterinarian's office, she relaxed on the examining table and merely glanced over her shoulder while the doctor listened to her heart and lungs.

"She certainly is easygoing," said Dr. Leali. "That must be the golden retriever in her."

"Is that just her disposition, then?" I said. "That's a relief! I was beginning to think she was retarded."

Velvet did, at times, behave like a normal puppy. I have a pair of mangled boots to prove it and—don't tell anyone— under the Lazy Boy, the area rug has a sizable stain. Now that Velvet has her adult teeth, however, and she's fully house trained, she's pretty easy to live with.

Velvet must think humans are a perverse lot, though. We fuss over a little wet spot on the carpet, but if we're watching TV when she wants out, we say, "Wait until the commercial."

Excuse me? Hel-LO-oh.

After five minutes of "just a minute" Velvet realizes we've tuned her out. When the polite "whuff" doesn't get our attention, Velvet hops on the couch and sticks her whiskers in Tom's face.

Velvet's technique for getting attention reminds me of

two different methods for spreading the message of salvation: some evangelizers are polite whuffers and others are whiskers-in-the-face types. Scripture indicates there's a place for both. Jesus sent his disciples out to spread the message into every town they could cover in a two-week period—whiskers-in-the-face evangelism. But Jesus also relates the parable about the persistent widow who presented her case before a certain judge every day—polite whuffing—until he finally listened to her.

I, like the widow in the parable, fall into the whuffer category. I'm always willing to answer questions about my faith, but I'm not assertive about initiating the topic of salvation. I pray that demonstrating consistent Christlike attitudes will encourage people to be more receptive to Christianity.

And I pray about particular people as well. I've been praying for Sandy for a couple of years. Sandy is agnostic and somewhat hostile toward organized religion. She doesn't understand that having a relationship with God and practicing organized religion are not the same thing. So at the first mention of anything spiritual, Sandy gets defensive.

I wondered, *Why would God place as restrained an evangelist as me in the path of someone as resistant as Sandy?*

Sandy knows that I believe Jesus is the Son of God and that he died so I might have eternal life. And I know I should always live what Jesus taught—love of neighbor, love of God. But around certain people, like Sandy, I'm especially careful to present a Christlike attitude. (Thank God I'm not around Sandy twenty-four hours a day!)

And I pray that Jesus will keep knocking at the door to Sandy's heart, that the Spirit of God will keep trying to enter.

And I'll keep praying—for a couple of years, for ten years…however long it takes. Like the widow, I'll be persistent in presenting my case to God, and I'll be persistent in the way I present myself to Sandy.

When Tom and I tune out Velvet, she gets in our faces because her need is urgent. There's a sense of urgency, too, in the minds of many evangelizers. But with a woman who has tuned out God, I'm praying that polite whuffing will get me farther than sticking my whiskers in her face.

Through patience a ruler can be persuaded,
and a gentle tongue can break a bone.
—Proverbs 25:15

Don't ask me why I treat Tom better.
—Velvet the dog

"Oh, sure," I said to Velvet. "Who gives you food and water? Who spends every waking moment making your life heaven on earth? Me! That's who." I was on a roll now. "And who do you make lovey-dovey with? Tom! That's who."

When Velvet was a puppy Tom was away from home a lot, so she had little opportunity to win his affection. Then too, Tom wasn't demonstrative toward Velvet. At that time he wasn't quite ready to relinquish his heart to a strange dog. So when Tom came home Velvet danced around his legs, and whenever he sat on the couch, she eased up next to him and laid her head in his lap.

Her behavior made me feel downright unappreciated (okay, jealous).

But Velvet's behavior also made me wonder about the way God interacts with people: For instance, why does someone who on the surface appears more unworthy sometimes seem to get special attention?

Beth is a case in point. When describing Beth, *Christlikeness* is not the first word that comes to mind. Beth burns the candle at both ends: parties, bars, sexy clothes, men—these are the things that matter to Beth. Still, she believes in God, and once she told me why.

"I'd lost my wallet," she told me. "My driver's license, all my credit cards, a couple of checks—just *everything* was in it. I looked everywhere—tore the house apart—and couldn't find it. I sat on the floor and cried and all of a sudden it came to my mind to pray. Which is real odd because I don't pray much.

"I guess I always believed in God, at least I would never say, 'There isn't any God,' but I never gave it much thought. That's why it's so funny it would come to my mind to pray. Anyway, I didn't exactly know how to say a prayer, so I said The Lord's Prayer. Then I said, 'If you're really there, God, please help me find my wallet. If you help me, I'll know there really is a God. Amen.'

"Then I got into the car to come to work, and I thought, *Look in the glove compartment.* My wallet was inside! Then I remembered I'd gone to the market, and I'd put my wallet in the glove compartment after I stopped at the video store."

"So now you believe in God?" I said.

"Well, I had to keep my promise," said Beth. "I said I'd believe, so now I have to believe."

At first I wasn't sure I believed Beth's story. Why would someone like Beth get such special attention from God?

Then I remembered a story in the Bible about two sons. The bad son left home to burn the candle at both ends while the good son stayed behind to help on the farm. After the bad son spent all his money and lost his friends, he had learned his lesson and came home to beg for help. In the meantime the father had provided for the needs of the good son, but when the bad son at last came home, he got special attention. For a time, the father placed his focus on the son who most needed attention.

Perhaps that's why our Heavenly Father paid attention to Beth: She prayed because of a material loss, but God perceived her spiritual need. And maybe that's why Velvet focused her attention on Tom: Because he spent time away from the pack, Velvet wanted to show him he was especially welcome.

It worked. Tom was soon won over by Velvet's charming advances.

Some animal behaviorists say pets can sense when someone has a special need. If Velvet directs her attention where it's especially needed, should I be surprised when God does the same thing?

[The] father said, "You and I are very close, and everything I have is yours. But . . . your brother . . . was lost and is found!"
—Luke 15:31–32 (TLB)

Whenever I discover something nice or nasty, they take it from me.   —Velvet the dog

One summer Velvet dug up something that smelled like moldy newspaper. I had no idea what it was, but Velvet seemed proud of her find. She shook it and tossed it around the yard until it dangled from her mouth in ragged chunks. Of course, I took it from her. If she swallowed some, it would no doubt end up a dark stain on my beige carpet.

A few days later, she dug up something quite different—about a half dozen oyster shells that looked like small, pearl fans. I took these from her too, but I cleaned them up and put them out for display on a shelf in the bathroom.

Velvet also collects ordinary objects—like sticks. I let her keep those because they're inoffensive and harmless, and not pretty enough to display on a bric-a-brac shelf. Basically, then, I make her give up the nice stuff or the nasty stuff and let her keep everything else.

My criteria for taking and leaving reminds me of the way some people look at morals. Some people reject the notion that there's any ultimate authority for judging what's nice or nasty behavior. So what one person considers evil behavior might be seen as acceptable to someone else, depending on the situation.

To those of us who say God sets the standards for niceness, the anything-goes culture says, "That's fine for you, but not everyone believes in God. So let's take God out of the morality equation." That, of course, takes away the quaint notion of sin. Sin, after all, has the nasty quality—like a dark stain on a beige carpet—of spoiling our view of ourselves and of the world we live in.

Moral tolerance, then, takes away both the spiritually nice and the spiritually nasty, and leaves nothing of value—no recognizable standard for niceness or nastiness.

Behaving without standards of right and wrong seems appealing—at first. But doing so would eventually erode the capacity for discernment. For instance, I felt pretty self-righteous when I turned in a wallet I found at Food-O-Rama . . . until I read about the little boy who returned $10,000 that had fallen from a Brinks truck.

On the other end of the scale, if I don't feel bad about not paying back that dollar I borrowed, then why not neglect to report some income to the IRS.

Living as if there were no standard of moral niceness toward which to strive prevents me from developing moral character—the ability to recognize the right thing and then do it even when no one is looking. And worse, with no definite limits on nastiness, how will I learn to recognize evil? Do-as-you-please morality blurs the line between good and evil; it eliminates both God and the devil.

Velvet is unable to recognize the harm in consuming nasty garbage. Nor is she able to discern the niceness of an oyster shell. Following a code of moral tolerance will eventually lead to the inability to recognize neither nastiness nor niceness.

And just as Velvet is quite content to play with an ordinary stick, those who follow the do-as-you-please culture content themselves with moral standards of no enduring value and are left holding nothing of significance.

In those days . . . every man did that which was right in his own eyes.
—Judges 17:6 (KJV)

He maketh me to lie down in pachysandra.
~Velvet the dog

Jake likes to lie under the shrubbery. Jake is my neighbor's dog, a brown and white springer spaniel, and he barks at my husband whenever Tom passes by on his regular walks. Jake is just doing his job—warning Tom to stay away and alerting his owners that someone is approaching.

Jake's owners planted a row of low shrubs along the front of their house, and on hot days Jake does his barking from a dark and cool spot under the bushes.

Velvet has her own cool retreats. On the north side of our house there's a bed of pachysandra, which is a shade-loving ground cover. After a few minutes of playing fetch on warm days, Velvet sprawls on her belly in the pachysandra. It's cool there in the shade of the eaves, and she pants and squints and recovers from her exercise.

Taking a break from the heat is a smart idea, but Velvet's behavior is merely instinctive. Left to their own devices, dogs will behave in their own best interests—they'll eat when they're hungry and drink when they're thirsty, sleep when they're tired and head for the shade when they're hot.

We humans, on the other hand, have learned to ignore our instincts, and often we don't rest and recover even when our bodies demand it.

I used to teach aerobics at a health club. Like most of the instructors at the club, I taught only two or three classes a week. But because I was the only instructor who did not also hold a full-time job or have small children at home, I was often the only one who was available to sub.

When I taught a lot of classes, my body became dehydrated and I'd get tired and irritable. But did I refuse when someone needed a sub? Oh, no. I didn't have the sense God gave a dog.

But I'm needed, I'd tell myself. *No one else is available ... my coworkers will be grateful . . . the club members will appreciate my sacrifice.* Right. The truth is, I wanted to be a hero. I wanted to indulge my pride. I wanted everybody to marvel at how much energy I still had after teaching eleven classes in a week.

My behavior was, of course, physically and emotionally unhealthy. Even Jesus took time out from serving to rest and recuperate. The Gospel of Luke says that Jesus often retreated to lonely places and prayed.

At the health club, I was serving the members, but my motives were not pure. Jesus didn't serve for recognition. He served to glorify God.

Animals, like people, sometimes place demands on themselves. Velvet plays fetch until her tongue hangs out the side of her mouth. And Jake races back and forth along the road at the edge of his owners' property barking his head off every time anyone walks by.

But Velvet and Jake know how to conserve their physical resources. When they've chased enough balls or barked enough at strangers, they take time out, retreat under a bush, or sprawl in the pachysandra.

God made both humans and canines. The difference is, dogs are content with their limitations. Humans, on the other hand, think we can ignore God's original performance specifications. We want to work longer and push harder and see results right now.

Jesus took time off, and I'm better at following Christ's example than I used to be. But a Christian is a work in progress, and I'm still tempted sometimes to push beyond my limits. But I try to remind myself: God is not interested in my list of accomplishments. He's interested in making me more like his Son.

[Jesus] said . . . "Come with me
by yourselves to a quiet place and get some rest."
~Mark 6:31

• COMMITTING TO GOD •

You can lead me to the water, but you can't make me jump in.
—Velvet the dog

"Come on," I said. "You'll love it!" Velvet didn't want to use her new wading pool.

Velvet had grown out of her fuzzy black puppy hair and into a long, silky coat. She looks like a golden retriever, except her fur is black, and she gleams in the sunshine. But that dark coat is warm in the summer, so I set up a child's plastic wading pool for her. She wasn't interested.

Coaxing didn't work, so I straddled her and wrapped my arms under her chest, then scootched over the pool. As soon as I set her down she backed out and shook water on me.

"What's the matter," I said. "You're a retriever. You're supposed to *like* the water."

Velvet gazed at me and didn't budge.

"The water's nice," I said. "See? It's clean, close to shore, no sharks."

My arguments did not impress her. When she was thirsty she lapped up some of the water, but she wouldn't use it to cool off. A few days later, though, after a long walk in warm weather, Velvet did step into the pool, and then she realized what she'd been missing. As Hamlet said, "The readiness is all."

For many years I approached God in the same way. As a teenager I'd accepted Christ as my Savior, but I'd never pursued a personal relationship with him. I had, like Velvet, sipped at the water but had never immersed myself. With hindsight, I can see that God was coaxing me to take the plunge. He sent messengers from time to time—not angels in the supernatural sense, but a young man at a management seminar who asked me if I knew Jesus; a female co-worker who set a godly example.

These "angels" helped me get my feet wet with a little information or Scripture. I was polite and told them that I was "saved." What I didn't say was that the event hadn't lived up to my expectations. I hadn't felt . . . well . . . spiritual.

And frankly, as I got older the whole idea seemed farfetched—a God who cared so much that he wanted to be involved in the smallest details of my life. And eternal life? That was unimaginable. I wanted to believe in the God of the Bible, but I didn't understand how such a God was possible. Like Velvet, I wasn't confident about making the plunge.

During that time I had dreams—different circumstances but the same theme; I made it through a treacherous environment but couldn't find my way back. One dream took place in a marshy area. The way through was easy, but when I was ready to return, I kept sinking; I couldn't find the solid path.

Then my mom got sick. We had long talks while I was taking care of her, and she told me many things—that she prayed for ordinary things, like to hear a certain song on the radio; that she believed in angels. Shortly after she died I was working on a project for a Christian publishing company, and I read four simple words: "Faith is a decision."

It then dawned on me how silly I'd been to think that belief in God was not authentic if I didn't feel it mystically descend on me. Faith that requires that kind of proof isn't— after all—faith. It was solely up to me whether or not to believe. And I couldn't think of a single good reason not to.

Velvet now uses her pool all the time until I put it away for the winter. She stands in it, sits in it, and in hot weather she lies down in it and her tail fans out on the surface.

The Bible says that Jesus is the Water of Life. Now that I've taken the plunge and committed myself to get closer to *him*, I find that water increasingly hospitable. The idea of eternal life still seems fantastic, but the more I read the Bible, the more I'm persuaded. The Gospel writers were either liars or lunatics—or totally convinced that Jesus was indeed the Living Water. And over the last two thousand years they've persuaded an awful lot of people to join them in the pool.

He leads me to quiet pools of fresh water.
He gives me new strength.
–Psalm 23:2-3 (GNB)

• DENYING SELF •

 Sometimes I gotta get a little water up my nose.
–Velvet the dog

I couldn't believe what I was seeing.

The weather was hot and humid, and a few moments earlier I'd filled Velvet's wading pool. While she stood in water up to her knees, I tossed her rubber ball into the pool, just to see what she'd do. She looked at it. I splashed the water a little. She looked at me.

"Well," I told her, "I can't stay here all day and coax you. I've got a sink full of dirty dishes and *dog hair* all over the livingroom carpet."

Velvet made a noise like, "uhUungh."

"I couldn't agree with you more," I said, and I went into the house.

A few minutes later I looked out the living room window, and Velvet was trying to pick up her ball. She bobbed for it like a kid bobbing for apples. She didn't like getting her face wet, but she shook her head then bobbed for it again and again until she finally got it.

Atta girl! I thought, and she tiptoed out of the pool and laid down in the grass. But then she sashayed back to the pool, dropped the ball into the water, and started bobbing all over again! For a dog, retrieving is instinctive, but for Velvet to follow her instincts in this particular instance meant overcoming her aversion to getting water up her nose.

The original disciples of Jesus also had to overcome their own aversions. Jesus told them that if they really wanted to follow him, they had to deny their natural inclinations—

Jesus called it taking up your cross (Matt. 16:24)—and face many difficulties. His disciples were willing, over and over again, to face all manner of trials to follow and to obey their *master*—to spread the word about a Person so important that history is divided at the time of his birth.

A man named Paul, for instance, underwent starvation, beatings, shipwreck—and that's just a few of his troubles—in order to tell the good news about Jesus. Paul's natural inclinations were probably to continue his life as a scholarly Pharisee—elegant dining, philosophical discussions, respect in the community—but Paul ran smack into Jesus. After that, Paul spent the rest of his life volunteering to get water up his nose, as over and over again he made the decision to deny himself and follow Christ.

I'll probably never have to worry about starving or getting beaten up for Jesus. For me, denying self means smiling when the cashier at Food-o-Rama is slow and I'm in a hurry. It means when I have a fender bender with the car, I thank God no one was injured instead of complain about the inconvenience.

No, no, no. I'm not always cheerful, or patient, or grateful. But I'm still a work in progress, and the process is everything. The process starts with Jesus, who is the Living Water. Like Velvet with her pool, I came to the water. Now, like my dog and like Paul, I have to bob for the ball. I expect I'll spend the rest of my life doing just that, struggling for self-denial, achieving it in one area, then struggling for it in another.

Because retrieving is natural to Velvet, she tolerates getting water up her nose. I, on the other hand, try to achieve what isn't at all natural to me—being nice when I don't feel nice, expressing gratitude when I don't feel grateful.

But God knows I don't like getting my face wet. He knows the price I pay every time I go back to the pool and struggle with that ball. So I like to imagine that, as I return to the water yet again, he watches from His livingroom window and, with a nod of approval, says, "Atta girl."

God holds us responsible . . . not for what we are,
but for what we might be.
–Edyth Draper

When the gate hangs open, the world looks very large.
—Velvet the dog

My husband, Tom, chuckled as he led Velvet into the kitchen. "She had an EHHH-xcellent adventure," he said. Velvet held her tail high and snorted, pleased as punch.

Velvet was six years old at the time, and three years earlier we'd fenced in a big area of the yard for her. Since the day we put up the fence, Velvet had never been outside her yard other than on a leash—until that morning in early spring. A deliveryman had left the gate open.

"Did she go out by the road?" I said, and Velvet headed for her dish.

"Nah," said Tom. A light snow had fallen during the night, and he pulled off his wet overshoes. "I followed her tracks. She didn't go far—out by the birdbath then back along the property line to the garage. I found her sniffing around the woodpile."

By this time Velvet had crunched down her breakfast and was licking her chops, right and left. Obviously, she'd forgotten the whole incident.

But I still shudder when I think about the busy road that runs by our house. And I'm surprised that, in the time she was free, Velvet hadn't wandered farther. I'd have thought she'd dash through the neighborhood and scatter everyone's garbage. Instead, she investigated the shrubbery close to home.

That incident got me to thinking about boundaries, about what they prevent and what they provide. Tom and I put up a fence to keep Velvet out of traffic. Likewise, when I was a kid my parents set limits—"Don't cross the street by yourself"—to keep me safe. But they also set boundaries so I'd learn self-discipline and how to make choices.

Safety and discipline are two results of boundaries, but I can think of one more. In college, my professor of classical literature, Mrs. Brown, allowed a creative project to replace one of our five-page essays. "The project must relate to the Trojan War," she said, "and must convey three aspects of Greek culture." Soon her desk was covered with board games, dolls in costume, and cassette tapes of dramatic readings.

She encouraged creativity by allowing freedom within boundaries—like drawing a square and saying, "Here's the perimeter, and inside you can do anything you want." The boundaries made us focus on the essentials, and the freedom allowed us to express those essentials in creative ways.

God also laid down a few boundaries. You know them: thou shalt not covet, thou shalt not commit adultery, and so on and so forth. They sound like a recipe for spoiling everyone's fun. But if we all followed those rules, life would be safer and a lot less stressful. No crime, no jilted spouses, no energy wasted lusting over my neighbor's restored Mustang convertible.

Velvet's fence provides safety; Mom and Dad's rules helped develop my character; Mrs. Brown's parameters encouraged creativity. God's commandments do all three: When I'm safe and if I possess self-discipline, I can be free to accomplish extraordinary things.

Absolute freedom for Velvet would place her in danger and would sure cause us trouble with the neighbors. And as Tom and I learned, she seemed insecure and unsure of herself when the gate was accidentally left open.

The world doesn't always provide a reliable set of parameters, and when we find an opening in the fence it's easy to become confused. When I stray outside of God's boundaries, however—when I envy or covet—the increase in my stress level and the decrease in my self-image tells me I'm in dangerous territory. And I realize all over again that God doesn't make rules to control us or hinder us, but to prepare us—for an excellent adventure.

Whoever looks closely into the perfect law that sets people free, who keeps on paying attention to it . . . will be blessed by God.
–James 1:25 (GNB)

• L O V I N G   G O D •

I never lose sight of my leader.
~Velvet the dog

Velvet likes the screened-in porch. The windows come almost to the floor, so she can sit by my chair and look outside and sniff the air coming through the screens. Even better from Velvet's point of view, when she's outside and I'm on the porch, she can always see me. Whether she's wading in her pool or patrolling the fence, she keeps me in her line of vision.

Velvet's behavior is not unusual. Dogs like to maintain contact with the pack leader. But no matter the reason, I'm touched that she's reassured by my presence. "I'm still here," I call out to her, and she resumes her doggy chores. If I go into the house to fold laundry or to answer the phone, within a few minutes Velvet yelps to be let in. Her leader is no longer in sight and she's anxious. The truth be told, I'm reassured by Velvet's presence, too. She is not only my early warning system, she's good company, and . . . well . . . I just plain like her.

Generally speaking, it's not hard to understand why dogs hang around people. Humans are a resource to dogs. We provide them with food and shelter, scratch their tummies, and give someone they can look up to. In ancient times dogs were, in turn, a resource to humans. They guarded the home, helped hunt for food, disposed of garbage, and pulled loads. These days, however, most people keep dogs solely as pets, and they've become a part of our families.

The modern relationship between humans and dogs is

somewhat parallel to the relationship between God and his children. Our need for God is evident: he created us, he sustains us, he provides strength and comfort, he answers prayer. In short, God is not only our primary resource, he is the Leader we look to for guidance and reassurance.

But as one might observe that most modern humans don't need dogs, one could also ask, "Why does God need humans?" He doesn't. And far brighter minds than mine have for thousands of years wondered why God created humans when he had no need of us.

Some theologians claim that God created us so we could glorify him. I feel sort of glorified when Velvet gazes at me as if I were a Rembrandt painting. But, the theologians point out, God doesn't need anyone to glorify him; he is infinitely holy regardless of human adoration. I, on the other hand, appreciate a little ego boost.

When it comes to comparing, though, how God relates to me and how I relate to Velvet, there is a common theme—love. God loves me, though he doesn't have to; I love Velvet though I don't have to. Velvet loves me partly because her instincts tell her I'm a resource, but mostly because it is a dog's nature to give love.

But when it comes to me loving God, the comparison breaks down. I have free will and can choose whether or not to love God. Many humans freely choose to not love him, and that's unfortunate. Because loving God not only impacts eternity, it enriches the here and now. When I chose to love God, the first benefit was the satisfaction I felt in my spirit that I'd made the right decision. Loving God fulfilled my longing for a meaning and a purpose in life.

On a practical level, loving God helps me to overcome bad habits, be more willing to forgive and to ask for forgiveness, in short, to approach all my relationships—with husband, family, friends, dogs—with a more loving attitude. And loving God has made me aware that, because God *is* love, he surely enriches my life in ways I'm not even aware of.

Some people might say that the way Velvet watches me while I sit on the porch shows a pathetic dependence. Not true. Canines have an instinctive need for a leader and are most content when they are serving someone they respect. Some people also might say that my dependence on God is pathetic. But dependence in humans is pathetic only when there is no choice.

As Velvet seeks to serve her leader, in a similar way I seek to serve my Leader, whom I have freely chosen to follow. And I try never to let him out of my sight.

Much of the wisdom . . . of the Creator appears in the several capacities and instincts of the creatures. . . . Surely we cannot but acknowledge God with wonder and thankfulness.
—Matthew Henry

I'll wait all day for you.
~Velvet the dog

Velvet knows how to wait.

If Tom takes a walk in the early evening, he sometimes doesn't take Velvet with him. At that time of day a lot of neighborhood dogs are out and Velvet is harder to handle. After he's been gone a few minutes, Velvet whines to be let out. Then she sits at the gate and gazes at the end of the driveway, waiting for Tom to come home.

Nor does she hold a grudge after he returns. As soon as she spies him coming up the drive, she stands up and swishes her tail. Then she prances around his legs when he comes through the gate. As soon as he speaks to her and touches her head, she goes about her doggy chores—patrolling the perimeter of the fence, whoofing at the tree tops—and, for all the world, appears like everything is hunky-dory.

I, on the other hand, am not good at waiting. When God was handing out patience, the bag was almost empty when he got to me. It's not the big things I have trouble waiting for. I've been praying about some things for a couple of years, which in God-time is about one nanosecond. But as I've become more spiritually mature I guess I've learned to tolerate God's timetable.

No, it's the little things that drive me crazy—waiting for microwave popcorn or for the car ahead of me to move on the green light, or for Tom to make his last-minute checks before we leave the house: toilet not running, lights out, burners turned off.

"I already did all that," I say.

"I'm just double checking," he says.

Sigh.

We're almost out the door and he turns back. "One more thing," he says.

SIGH!

I stand with one hand on the doorknob and tap my foot and gaze at the ceiling...and wait.   Note: I didn't say wait *patiently*.

After say, twenty seconds, I go in search of Tom. In a tight and high-pitched voice I say, "What *are* you doing?"

He smiles and touches my shoulder, "Just checking the steam iron."

I push his hand away and, later, the mood in the car is strained, until I acknowledge there'll be no cosmic upheaval because we're delayed five minutes getting to the grocery store. Then to diffuse the tension I say something like, "My goodness, look how many cars are parked at the bank."

Why do I lose my patience over trivial delays? Why don't I just take them in stride?

Perhaps I should analyze the situation. When I'm waiting for Tom to finish his check list: (1) I feel insulted because he thinks it's okay to make me wait; (2) I feel insulted that he doesn't trust me (I told him I checked all that stuff); (3) I feel odd just doing nothing (there's not enough time to start something like scouring the kitchen sink).

Perhaps I should consider the way God created dogs, and take a clue from Velvet. Except I'm not much good at gazing after Tom with an adoring and expectant look on my face.

But, unlike me, Velvet doesn't mind doing nothing while she waits. She doesn't get impatient or feel insulted. And when Tom returns she doesn't shrug off his touch and sulk for ten minutes. And she never has to diffuse a tense situation.

That Velvet. She just doesn't know how to handle men! We have bought into the cultural myth that when we're waiting, we're doing nothing.

> *... If we can't be still and wait, we can't become what God created us to be.*
> *—Sue Monk Kidd quoting an unidentified monk*

I'll take your last bite, but don't expect gratitude.
~Velvet the dog

I have only myself to blame—I'm such a pushover. When Velvet watches me eat, she leans forward with her ears cocked at attention and her eyes like marbles. The overall effect fairly screams, "If I don't get just one teensy-weensy nibble of that turkey sandwich I'll have a stroke." To add to the drama, she drools.

Of course I give in and hand her my last bite. But if I expect any show of gratitude I'm sadly disappointed. With the meat still between her teeth, she trots over to see what Tom is eating. She plops her bottom in front of him and assumes the same pose she used on me. At that moment the earth could open up and swallow me and Velvet wouldn't notice.

When I feel like I've been had by Velvet, I imagine how God felt toward the Old Testament nation of Israel. They appealed to God whenever they wanted something. When Egypt enslaved them, they cried out to God to free them. When they were hungry and thirsty in the desert, they complained to God and he provided food and water. When they were tired of wandering in the wilderness, God led them to a valuable piece of real estate.

Like Velvet eagerly taking the last bite of my sandwich, so Israel accepted everything God offered them. And like Velvet turning away from me to see what Tom had to offer, Israel turned from God and sought the favor of false idols.

But I've no business pointing an accusing finger at

Israel's idol worshipers. While I don't bow down before a golden statue, I do, however, let work—or watching TV, or even my own desire to be liked—come before God.

If I've stayed up late or if I have a lot of work to do, I put off reading my Bible and praying. Nor do I get up a few minutes early in the morning to spend time with God. No. I usually pray or read my Bible when the "high-priority" tasks are finished.

And do I make a point of speaking openly about my Savior? Doing that might offend someone or make someone uncomfortable. I don't want to come off like a religious whacko. I want people to like me.

The apostle Paul and his colleagues weren't concerned about popularity. They experienced severe persecution when they tried to spread the word about salvation in Christ. They were at various times stoned, beaten, whipped, and thrown into prison because they gave Christ the highest priority in their lives.

And here I am, living in a country where I can say almost anything without fear. I could proclaim the message of Jesus Christ in the middle of the sidewalk and probably not incur even a fine.

I take the good things God has provided for me—a comfortable house, abundant food, decent clothing—then turn from him and bow down to the god of fitting in. Popularity has a higher priority than obeying my Savior: "Go into all the world and preach the good news to all creation. Whoever believes . . . will be saved" (Mark 16:15-16).

Sometimes I wonder why God continues to bless me. Perhaps he looks at me the way I look at my dog. Velvet's instincts dictate that she look after her own best interests. I know that she loves me, and even if she is sometimes fickle I realize that Velvet is, after all, only a dog.

I don't express my gratitude for God's blessings by aggressively spreading the message about Jesus, but perhaps God looks into my heart rather than at my behavior. And because nothing is impossible for God, maybe he will devise other methods for me to achieve his will. After all, God knows that I'm only human.

It's the Holy Spirit's style to fashion holy lives among the inept.
–Eugene Peterson

You expect me to eat that?
–Velvet the dog

When I'm eating, Velvet stares at me as if she were starving. Her eyes plead for just one teensy-weensy bite of my sandwich. Except in this instance, I'm not eating a sandwich. I'm eating an apple. And when I offer her the core, her whole attitude changes. A chunk of tart fruit is obviously not what she expected. She cranes her neck forward and sniffs, then curls back her top lip and takes hold of the core by a tiny piece of skin. After one half-hearted chew, she spits it out.

So I pick up the apple and stick it in her face. "You little brat! I thought you were hungry." With just the slightest lift of her chin Velvet turns her head away, and if a dog could sneer, she'd say, "You expect me to eat *that*?"

"Well," I say, "I'm sorry it's not a roast beef sandwich!" Sarcasm is wasted on a dog.

The Pharisees of Jesus' day were a little like Velvet. Just as she seemed by all appearances to truly desire food, the Pharisees put on a great show of desiring to be filled with holiness. In reality, though, the Pharisees were not truly hungry for the things of God.

When they encountered real holiness—the very Son of God—and he offered them bitter fruit, they, like Velvet, were not prepared to swallow it. All of Israel expected a warrior Messiah who would redeem the political power of their nation. But this man Jesus was a humble carpenter who taught that the kingdom of God was one of peace and love for humankind. And he preached that those who placed too high a value on wealth and position risked forfeiting that kingdom.

The Pharisees anticipated a messiah carrying a platter of roast beef, and instead they were given one who offered them an apple core. As it turns out, they weren't that hungry.

The Pharisees remind me a little of myself. As a teenager I "got saved," but I never really drew close to God, nor did I think about pursuing the things of God. I just wanted to feel like I was part of something, and the people in church made me feel welcome.

I joined the choir and the church orchestra, attended church services and Sunday school, went along on skating parties, retreats, fellowship gatherings, songfests, picnics, etc., etc., etc. By all appearances, it sure looked like I was becoming holy, but in reality I knew nothing about a personal relationship with God.

Sure, the church asked me to give up a few things, but that bitter apple wasn't hard to swallow as long as I was having fun with my friends. When I smelled roast beef, though, I was ready to spit out the apple core. An opportunity arose to fit in with a group outside the church—a group who didn't expect me to give up anything or to get up early on Sunday mornings.

Now that I'm all grown up, I realize that filling up on the things of God does not mean settling for apple cores. When I turn to God for sustenance—whether in prayer to help me overcome pride, or to the Bible for a study in human nature—my plate is full.

So in one way, I'm still like Velvet. She turned her nose up at apples because she wasn't really hungry. If she couldn't get roast beef, she preferred dog food over tart fruit, and her dish was always full. Likewise, when God is my main dish, I never worry about my appetite going unsatisfied.

Give us this day our daily bread.
~Matthew 6:11 (KJV)

I arrange what's important around my rock.
~Velvet the dog

"Where did *this* come from?" Tom was padding around the house in his slippers and had stepped on a rock.

"Velvet brought it in," I said. "She picked it out of the pachysandra bed. I try to make her keep her rocks outside, but sometimes she slips one past me."

The pachysandra runs along one side of the house, inside the fenced-in yard. The bed is edged with railroad ties and the ground beneath the plants is covered with rocks. The rocks are more or less the size of golf balls—just right for Velvet to carry around in her mouth.

The problem is she doesn't put them back. We have to pick them up before we mow, and sometimes Velvet carries one into the house. Besides, she could damage a tooth, playing with a rock. So as of this writing we're in the process of disposing of the railroad ties and the rocks and replacing the pachysandra with perennials.

Velvet has a couple of toys that stay outside, and she occasionally picks up a bit of debris. One day she had gathered her various possessions—toys, a stick, a mangled cardboard cylinder—into one place in the yard. In the center of the collection was a rock.

I saw a certain symbolism in her arrangement: Velvet's important possessions were arranged around her rock. God—the Rock—should be the center of my life, and everything else—possessions, work, relationships—should be arranged around him. At one time I placed myself—my ambitions, my impulses, my obsessions—at the center of my existence. I still occasionally lose focus, but the effort to conduct my life with God at the center has made a difference.

When I acknowledge that all my possessions ultimately come from God, I grasp them less tightly and do not allow them to possess me. I used to brag when I bought something new, and I felt embarrassed that my neighbors had nicer possessions than I. With God at the center, I'm grateful that I lack nothing. Money and possessions are no longer ends in themselves and I'm more satisfied with what I have.

At one time I worked in an office with other employees, but now I'm a freelancer and, as such, in a fortunate position. I work mostly on projects that are God-centered in subject matter. But I also tutor at a community college and do some volunteer work. With God at the center of all my work, the way I interact with my coworkers has changed. I'm more conscientious about avoiding gossip, office politics, fraternization with the opposite sex, and passing judgment on my colleagues.

Having God at my center impacts relationships other than those at work. God's way is for me to place others before myself—a practice that definitely goes against my grain. So showing more consideration to others is something I implemented a little at a time, starting with my husband. I asked him for advice, offered more help on do-it-yourself projects, let him have the last chocolate donut (that really hurt!). It's not hard to guess the results: a more harmonious household. And now my husband shows more consideration to me!

Velvet put a rock at the center of her important possessions, but doing so was not the result of forethought. Placing the Rock at *my* center, however, took effort. And I admit that, initially, I resented suppressing my ego. (Okay, sometimes I still resent it.) Funny, though, how doing things God's way has worked out. The small considerations I extend to others cost me very little, and I've reaped far more than I've invested. You might say that by putting myself last, I'm really first. It works out so well you'd think it was planned that way.

God's love [doesn't] demand change; it produces change.
—Les Parrott

Sometimes a pup needs to remember who's boss.
~Velvet the dog

"You picked out Velvet," Tom said. "I want to pick out Buster."

When Tom was a kid, he had a dog named Buster. But he and his mother, a widow, moved into a housing project that didn't allow pets. So his Buster went to live with Aunt Julie. Now Tom wanted to choose a dog to replace the pet he'd lost.

"What kind of dog are you looking for?" I said. We'd strolled past every cage at the humane society, and with each puppy we looked at Tom grew more disappointed.

"I don't know," he said. "I'll know Buster when I see 'im." He paused in front of a three-month-old golden retriever mix and sighed. "Maybe this one."

I gestured to Susan, the attendant. She started to open the cage then paused. "If you like goldens," said Susan, "we have a six-week-old golden mix in a separate holding area. Would you like to see her?"

We followed Susan through a maze of halls and doorways. "I'm taking you the long way," she said, "to avoid the euthanizing area."

A small cage in the holding area contained one very small puppy. "She was brought in just last night," said Susan, and she carefully lifted the puppy. "Someone found her on a country lane—probably got dumped off."

Susan placed the puppy in my arms. Her coat was very light, almost white, and a smear of excrement stained one ear. She weighed almost nothing, and I could feel every bone in her body. I was sure that Tom would hesitate about caring for a creature so fragile.

I gently transferred the puppy into Tom's arms. My husband is a large-boned man, and he was wearing a huge, down-filled coat. When he held the puppy, I saw only her great, dark eyes peering over his elbow. Tom rubbed the top of her head with two fingers. "This is Buster," he said.

Buster's delicate appearance was deceiving. Her sad eyes and cute little face disguised the personality of a storm trooper. As soon as we put her on the floor at home she waddled over and crunched down Velvet's dog food, then dragged Velvet's bone-on-a-rope under the diningroom table. Velvet just grinned and wagged.

At the time I thought, *I can't believe Velvet is so tolerant of this little usurper.*

After Buster had been in the family for a few weeks, we were all playing catch outside. I threw the ball; Velvet sprinted out to retrieve it. Buster pranced up and tried to grab the ball from Velvet's mouth. Without even breaking stride, Velvet tumbled Buster with a swing of her head and then brought the ball to me. Tolerance, it seems, extends only so far.

Velvet's forbearance toward Buster is a little like God's indulgence toward me. When I get like Buster, charging headlong, anxious to show what I can do, God knows it's time to send me tumbling. When recently I joined an informal writer's group, I'd already been published. My poetry had received public attention, so I was anxious to dazzle the group with my work. Before I got a chance to show off, an unassuming lady in the group read her essay, a vivid and poignant childhood memory about "Harry, the Dump Man."

I was humbled—and then grateful I hadn't made a fool of

myself by boasting. With a flick of her nose, Velvet chastises Buster. With even less effort, God brings me down to earth. And then when I acknowledge who's in charge, he faithfully upholds me. How great is thy faithfulness.

The grace of God can live with some people
with whom no one else could ever live.
—Jonathan Edwards

God made me cute for a reason.
~Buster the puppy

The X-ray technician probably just wanted to help me relax. I was there for my routine mammogram, and when I told Jan that my husband and I just adopted a new puppy she told me her own puppy story.

"We just got a beagle puppy," she said. "As soon as the lights were out that first night, the puppy started crying. So my little boy, Brian, took the puppy downstairs to the rec room so the noise wouldn't bother the rest of the family.

"That puppy must have cried all night long. The next morning Brian came upstairs. His eyes were bloodshot, with dark circles under them. I could tell he was at the end of his rope.

"He looked at me and said, 'Mom, now I know why God made puppies so cute!'"

The first night we had Buster was no picnic either. We spread newspapers on the bedroom floor and closed the door. Then we turned out the lights and waited to see what would happen.

Velvet always sleeps in our bedroom, on the floor by my side of the bed. That first night the tiny puppy, in an unfamiliar situation, wanted to stay close to the one she recognized as her own kind. But Velvet wanted nothing to do with a puppy. Buster scampered across the newspapers to be near Velvet—kitcha-kitcha-kitcha; Velvet moved away—keech-keech-keech. For the rest of the night it was kitcha-kitcha-kitcha; keech-keech-keech; kitcha-kitcha-kitcha; keech-keech-keech.

Fortunately, a new puppy adapts quickly. Soon, Buster didn't need the newspapers, and she didn't need Velvet to feel secure at night. We willingly tolerated some minor annoyances for a short time, partly because Buster was so helpless and adorable.

Tolerating the annoying behavior of humans is a little harder. My husband is a case in point. Tom likes to make stacks. The mail-to-look-at-right-away stack. The mail-to-look-at-later stack. The catalogs-I-may-order-from stack. The papers-I-don't-know-what-to-do-with stack. There are piles of stuff on the coffee table, piles on the end table, piles on the bookcase, the dinner table, the chair in the corner.

I bought a filing cabinet, thinking Tom could make files for his piles and put them out of sight. Now there are piles on top of the filing cabinet!

Tom has many wonderful qualities, but at times I forget them and feel resentful over petty annoyances. But somewhere I read . . . or heard . . . if you want to change the way you feel about someone, pray for that person.

I began to pray regularly for Tom—thanking God for my husband, asking God to keep him safe, and to help him feel God's love. I won't say that suddenly every little irritation became a source of delight, nor did I look at the living room and praise God for all the clutter. But when the stacks of stuff irritated me, even though I had not prayed about that specific annoyance, I remembered my husband's wonderful qualities: he cares about doing the right thing, he works hard to provide for us, he encourages me in my pursuits, he makes me laugh. And at times he is—yes—quite adorable.

Puppies are sometimes annoying but they're so cute and entertaining that it's easy to forgive them. When my husband starts a new pile I sigh and shake my head, but I try to remember his good qualities far outweigh the minor annoy-ances. Besides, there's an outside chance that Tom may sometimes find me irritating. So I'll continue to pray for my husband—not because it changes him, but because it has changed me.

For all right judgment of any man, it is useful, nay essential, to see his good qualities before pronouncing on his bad.
~Thomas Carlyle

I never lower my tail.
~Buster the puppy

"How does Velvet get along with Buster?" Dr. Leali said. "Well . . ."

Buster had been with us only a few days, and Tom and I had taken her to the veterinarian for an examination and to start her puppy shots. She weighed in at four pounds, and she needed worming and flea treatment. Because Buster was undernourished, Dr. Leali advised how and what to feed her, then asked how the two dogs tolerated one another.

"Buster's making herself right at home," I said, "but Velvet's not exactly pleased. She snaps and growls a lot."

Dr. Leali chuckled. "That's pretty typical behavior for the established dog. But Buster has to learn her place in the pack. Unless it looks like Velvet is hurting the puppy, let them work things out between them."

The veterinarian was right, and the two dogs spent a couple of weeks adjusting to each other. It went something like this: Velvet lies down near a dog toy. Buster waddles over to play with Velvet and the toy. Buster tugs on the toy then Velvet lunges and bellows at her. Velvet never actually laid a tooth on the puppy, but sometimes Buster got blown off her feet from the velocity of Velvet's bark.

Buster, though, didn't make fearful little yips or tuck her tail and run away. Instead, she yapped right back. Buster was about the size of Velvet's head, but the little pup stood up to Velvet and matched her yap for bark.

Buster reminds me of Abraham in the Old Testament when he haggled with God. God said he would destroy the town of Sodom because of its wickedness, but Abraham's nephew Lot lived in that city. So Abraham pestered God into sparing the life of Lot.

I'm filled with wonder that a mere human had the nerve to press negotiations with the Almighty. I can imagine the following scenario:

God turns toward Sodom, and Abraham approaches the Creator: "Will you spare the city if you find fifty good people living there?"

God faces Abraham, but meets a steady gaze. "You've got spunk, Abraham," God says. "Okay, I'll spare Sodom if I find fifty good people there."

Abraham scurries after God: "But Lord," says Abraham, "what if there are only forty good people?"

God spins on Abraham and scowls: "Abraham! There's a fine line between spunk and folly. But okay, forty good people."

As God again turns toward Sodom he hears Abraham right at his heels. God whirls on Abraham with such force that the man is blown over. But, unharmed, Abraham springs to his feet. "What if," says Abraham, "only ten good people can be found in Sodom?"

God clamps his lips and his eyes flame; all creation holds its breath . . . then God explodes in laughter.

I have to admire Abraham even while I puzzle over his apparent foolhardiness. In the same way, I admire and puzzle over Buster when she's in-your-face with Velvet. Both the puppy and the patriarch seem to tempt fate by facing off with a being who is much more powerful than they.

Although Buster and Abraham both earn my admiration, I learn two quite different lessons from them: Abraham reminds me that I can press my case before God without fear; Buster reminds me that I may not always get what I want.

God . . . allows their voice to be heard in the court of heaven.
–NIV text commentary

I love my humans but, oh, that Velvet.
—Buster the puppy

Buster is playing with a piece of broccoli. It fell on the kitchen floor while I was fixing a stir fry, and she picked it up and trotted off to the sofa. It's two hours later, and she's still playing with that wilted chunk of vegetable, even though there's a fortune in dog toys lying all over the house.

I don't always understand dog behavior. Buster might be lying on the sofa, perfectly content, then it's as if she suddenly thinks, *Oh my gosh. My rubber bone is in the bedroom and I want it here.* She jumps down, trots off to the other room, and carries her toy back to the sofa.

At other times, Buster just sits and stares at me. What does it mean? What does she want? Some experts say that what a dog really wants is to be with other dogs.

When Buster first came to live with us, she attached herself to black Velvet like a blond shadow. She played with whatever Velvet played with, slept where Velvet slept, and did her jobs where Velvet did her jobs.

For the first couple of weeks Velvet was cool toward the puppy. Then she experienced what might be described as a canine epiphany. Velvet realized that playing chase-me or tug-of-war with Buster involved more subtlety and more communication than playing with me. Humph.

Oh, sure. They come to me to be petted and fussed over, but they understand each other better than they understand me, and far better than I understand them.

Humans, too, have a need to be understood by other humans. But imagine what it would be like to have nothing in common with anyone: for a dog—a pack animal—to live in total isolation. Or for an especially gifted person—say, a molecular engineer—to never encounter anyone else who could identify with his or her specialty.

Seems to me that kind of isolation would have been the experience of Jesus. True, he had twelve close friends with whom he lived for three years, but while Jesus was among them, these men never understood what kind of being he was (John 14:9), nor did they comprehend a great deal of what He said (Mark 8:17).

Once, however, a centurion came to Jesus asking him to heal an ailing servant. The centurion knew instinctively that, with only a word from Jesus, the servant would be healed. "For I myself," said the centurion, "am a man under authority, with soldiers under me" (Matt. 8:9). The centurion recognized that Jesus, too, both gave and took orders; that although he had power over demons and diseases, he obeyed a higher power.

The Bible says that Jesus was astonished at the centurion's great faith (v. 10). But I wonder if Jesus was not also astonished at meeting someone who understood the Savior's position.

Perhaps this is wishful thinking on my part, for who else on earth could empathize with Jesus, with his fatigue, his frustrations, his sorrow? With whom could he discuss his crucial spiritual mission? No one on earth—only the Father.

Truth is, I don't even understand my dogs sometimes. I'm glad, though, they understand each other. I'm glad, too, that I have friends who empathize with me, and a husband who knows me better than I sometimes know myself. And what my friends or my husband doesn't understand, I know that God does. He understands me—and my dogs. I'll bet he even understands why Buster plays with wilted vegetables.

This is the hunger we all have—to be liked,
to be loved, to share our love and lives.
–Delores Curran

Down is harder than up.
~Buster the puppy

Buster was attached to my ankle.

"Look," I said to Tom, and pointed down. "This puppy is no bigger than my foot and she has my whole ankle in her mouth."

Tom lowered the paper and grinned. "That's my Buster," he said. "She's Superpuppy."

Indeed.

From the moment we carried Buster home from the humane society and her little pink paws touched down on the kitchen carpet, she was primed for adventure.

Although nothing got in her way, for the first few days Buster had difficulty negotiating the front steps when it was time to go out. So we carried her down, then after she did her job she waddled over to the steps and tried to climb up. At first we gave her a little boost in the hindquarters, but about day three Tom came in from outdoors, grinning from ear to ear. "Buster came up the steps all by herself!"

Obviously, this was a most remarkable puppy.

The next trip outside, I let her try going down the steps; she inched over the edge of the porch until she was rump over shoulders, then she backed up and gazed at me. Going down was still too scary, and she whimpered for help.

I thought, *Life is a little like that. The ups are easier than the downs.* Obviously, it's easy to praise God in times of extraordinary good fortune—like when my first article was published. And I'm certain to lean on God during extraordinary difficulties like undergoing surgery.

But I also have ordinary ups and downs—ups like when the car keeps working day after day, and when I have just enough leftovers to make supper. And downs like when a lid is stuck, so I yank it off and pickle juice splashes on my blouse.

When the majority of my life consists of ordinary up events, I tend to get complacent and congratulate myself; I must be doing everything right. Not likely. Like Buster when she needed a little boost up the steps, I do not create even the little ups by myself. And when the ordinary downs happen, well, life is full of little mishaps, and it seems frivolous to call on God to loosen a stuck jar lid. Still, it doesn't seem God would feel put upon if I took a deep breath and thought, *God help me be strong and stay calm.* Surely God constantly upholds me, not just in times of extraordinary fortune or extraordinary difficulties, but through the ordinary ups and downs as well.

Puppies grow too quickly, and within a week Buster learned to hop down the steps one at a time, her little brown ears flopping at each descent. There was no time, however, to mark the passage of that milestone. She immediately toddled over to a pine branch ten times her size and tried to drag it into the house. When I offered her a smaller stick she dashed away and got tangled up in the rose bushes.

Buster's little adventures are the ordinary ups and downs in the life of a puppy, and she remains blissfully unaware of why her life is pleasant and safe. In a similar way, I forget to be thankful that the car didn't break down on the freeway, and I am often not mindful that God is always present, even when I open a pickle jar.

And that's when I most need God to help me remember—even an ordinary day is a day full of help and blessings.

The Lord thy God shall bless thee in all that thou doest.
—Deuteronomy 15:18 (KJV)

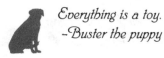
Everything is a toy.
–Buster the puppy

Buster sure knows how to have a good time. She was puny when we first brought her home from the humane society, but after a couple of weeks of gaining both weight and energy, she seemed to delight in mischief—especially getting into it right under my nose. Terry cloth held some special fascination for her.

I hung a dishtowel through the handle of the drawer nearest the kitchen sink, and one end dangled about eighteen inches above the floor. Buster liked to grab the hanging end and tug on it until the towel jerked off the handle. But she was still small and her getaway was hampered. The towel dragged between her legs as she trotted away, and she tripped over it.

Then Buster discovered the terry face cloth. After I wash my face in the evening, I hang the wash cloth over the edge of the bathtub to dry. When I applied face lotion, Buster grabbed the wash cloth. I caught only a glimpse as she high-tailed it, chin up and ears back, down the hall.

Buster turns almost anything—even terry cloth—into a toy. I chase her down and relieve her of the ill-gotten booty, and she makes sad eyes—for about four seconds—and then snuffles around for something else to get into.

Mischief and joy are part of a puppy's nature and Buster doesn't spend much time moping over the injustice of life. Enjoying the simple things and maintaining a joyful outlook have obvious human applications.

After my mom died, sentiments like "It's God's will," or "She's in a better place" quite frankly made me cringe. Well-meaning people seem to think cliches somehow take the edge off grief.

It was Mother's own words—those spoken during her last few weeks of life—that offered me the most comfort. She had talked about guardian angels and about how God answered some of her prayers. During that same period I happened to be reading a couple of books about angels and about heaven. I say, "happened to be reading," but I don't think it was coincidence. I feel those particular books were placed in my hands for a reason.

God met me at the place I needed him, and then in his own way and in his own time, he drew me closer to him. After Mom died I did not receive instant healing, but I did find myself seeking God more earnestly, and he did give me comfort—through simple things.

I first realized that on an evening in late summer. I was walking with a friend, and I lifted my head for some reason—to sigh or straighten my back. The sky was very blue and very clear, and it seemed like this was the first time I'd really looked at the sky all summer. In the east, a haze of nimbus clouds drifted just above the horizon, and they were tinted a light salmon by the setting sun.

"Look," I said to my friend. "Maybe it's my imagination, but the clouds seem more beautiful this year."

"Maybe," she said, "you're just starting to look up more."

I wonder if my friend was aware of her insight. I'd been preoccupied with grief, looking inward. And that evening I realized I was being restored, because I'd begun looking up—to God.

It's a bit of a stretch to compare Buster, having fun with

pieces of cloth, to me, sensing the presence of God on a summer evening. But we both received joy from simple things. That ability comes naturally to puppies. I, on the other hand, needed help, and I got it by looking up.

Teach us delight in simple things. . .
–Rudyard Kipling

I'm a mystery sometimes, but I'm never boring.
~Buster the puppy

It's hard to stay angry at a puppy. I wagged my finger under Buster's nose: "No! No! No! Stay out of the waste basket!" And a few seconds later I bent over to stroke her silky brown ears: "Isn't that cute. She's napping with my old slipper."

When she was awake, though, Buster was busy, busy, busy. She tugged at the fringe on the rug; she sneaked into the closet and chewed on my brown loafers; she nipped at Velvet's ankles.

These antics are cute in a little puppy, but Buster was part yellow lab and she would grow into a sizable dog. I made a mental note: Sign up to take Buster to obedience school. This dog was going to be a challenge, but she would never be boring.

She not only tried my patience, but her behavior was sometimes puzzling.

For three or four months, Buster slept under our bed every night. Since dogs are creatures of habit, I figured Buster would sleep in that same place every night for the rest of her life.

But one evening about nine o'clock Buster asked to go out. When I opened the door to the porch, she went to her cushion and laid down. Before I went to bed I checked on her. "Do you want to come in?" I said. She lifted her head but settled back down and heaved a great sigh. So for the next couple of months, Buster slept on the porch every night.

I was puzzled by her behavior, but if that's what made her happy . . .

Buster seems like an uncomplicated creature, but she's equipped with a whole set of instincts and behaviors I don't understand. Even the experts—the behaviorists and zoologists—don't have an explanation for every move a dog makes.

So if I sometimes can't figure out my dog, it's no wonder I don't understand God. When I read my Bible, one question in particular keeps puzzling me: Why does God in the Old Testament seem so different from God in the New Testament?

In the Old Testament, God delivers stern and wrathful judgment. He decreed the death penalty for any number of transgressions, from adultery to gathering firewood on the Sabbath. One time, in the book of Numbers, God caused a whole household—women, children, and servants—to be swallowed up by a big crack in the earth.

Then in the New Testament I read about Jesus. He said, "I and the father are one," but Jesus seems far removed from the God of the Old Testament. Rather than stoning an adulteress, Jesus forgives her and sends her on her way. Another time he defends his disciples for gathering wheat on the Sabbath.

But just when I think the old God has turned over a new leaf, he pops up again in the New Testament: Ananias and Saphira are struck dead because they told a lie.

Frankly, I'm confused, and God's apparent contradictions in behavior are embarrassing when I'm confronted by a skeptic. "Your God is supposed to be perfect and unchanging," says the doubter, "so how do you explain these changes?" Well—I can't. If even the experts—the theologians and the philosophers—don't have all the answers, I certainly don't.

But then I remember my dog Buster. I don't know why she's sometimes unpredictable, but still I trust her instincts. If she barks out the window, for instance, I check to see what's happening out there. Likewise, I don't understand all the ways of God. Studying the Bible, reading relevant books, and praying add to my understanding, but I've long since decided that I don't have to know everything about God before I'll put my trust in him.

And I trust, too, that God will not be offended if I say he and Buster have one thing in common: neither are ever boring.

Can you fathom the mysteries of God?
Can you probe the limits of the Almighty?
—Job 11:7

I'm a manipulator, but ya gotta love me!
~Buster the puppy

Buster is one sneaky pup. I scolded her once when I caught her grabbing the wash cloth off the edge of the bathtub. After that she waited until my back was turned before she grabbed it. Ditto with the toilet paper, my socks, and my toast off the coffee table.

Buster is not only sneaky, she is sometimes manipulative. After she'd learned to scratch at the door to be let out, it didn't take her long to connect scratching at the door with moving humans off the couch. This is a useful skill to Buster, especially if one of us humans is on the couch and cuddling Velvet instead of Buster.

Tom and I thought we were imagining things at first, but we recognized the scenario after about three times. (It seems humans do not grasp certain concepts as quickly as puppies do.)

The sequence of events goes something like this: Velvet has her head on my lap. Buster assesses situation then sits on floor and whines. Human says, "Gotta go out?" Buster's ears work as she communicates, "No, you dolt. I want to be where Velvet is." Human ignores Buster. Buster trots to kitchen and scratches at door. Human gets off couch and opens door. Buster trots back to couch and hops onto now vacant spot.

Buster reminds me of a man named Jacob who also had manipulative and deceitful streaks. Jacob manipulated his older brother out of the family inheritance then later tricked his father into giving him a special blessing. Those two tricks got him banished to his uncle's home, where Jacob tricked his uncle and wound up with a large herd of livestock. This is not the plot of an afternoon soap opera. It's a story from the Bible, and you can read it in the book of Genesis starting about the middle of chapter 25.

Despite Jacob's trickery, God made a covenant with him—to bless him and make him the father of a nation. So even though Jacob was tricky, God used him for a great good—to found Israel, the nation of people who were the ancestors of Jesus.

Why would a scamp like Jacob be chosen for such an important destiny? If God had waited for a perfectly right-eous person to come along, we'd still be waiting for the first coming of Christ. But God loved Jacob and granted him this unmerited privilege, not in spite of Jacob's character flaws, but to produce a change in his flawed character. And though God loves everyone, he had a special purpose for the Hebrews, his chosen people, and the promise he made to Jacob laid the foundation to that purpose.

In a similar way, I made a bargain with the humane society to give Buster a good home—even though she has turned out to be a sneaky little rascal. Beyond any agreement, though, I just plain love Buster and I know that her wiley ways spring from natural instincts.

I know that God doesn't perceive me like I perceive Buster: "She has her faults, but she's such a cute little rascal and it is, after all, in her nature to misbehave now and then." No, my misdeeds are not perceived so lightly; they have after all extracted a very high price.

But the story of Jacob gives me hope that God has a purpose for even the most flawed of his children, and when I see how Buster enhances our lives—she's good company and she makes me laugh; she loves Tom and me and she's a companion for Velvet—I'm convinced that God can use all his creatures to create good. And if God can do it with a dog, surely he can do it with me.

One may not doubt that, somehow, good shall come of water and of mud.
—Rupert Brooke

• GOD'S STEADFASTNESS •

I'm a rascal, but you signed a contract.
—Buster the puppy

Unfortunately, the latest style in footwear does not feature tooth marks. Without thinking, I left the closet door open, so thanks to Buster . . .

Puppies like to chew, and my dogs have all kinds of chew toys. Buster, however, prefers to explore different textures. I once left the cabinet door under the bathroom sink ajar. When I climbed out of the shower I saw the door hanging wide open, so I threw on a bathrobe and padded off to find Buster. She was curled up on the couch in the living room surrounded by mounds of shredded toilet paper.

After that I stretched rubber bands between the knobs on the cabinet doors to keep them closed. The next time I was in the shower I heard a muffled thud. I peeked around the shower curtain just in time to see Buster trot off with another roll of toilet paper. She'd managed to pry open the cabinet door in spite of the rubber bands.

Buster never destroyed anything that couldn't be replaced, but what if she had? Tom and I signed an agreement with the humane society that outlined our responsibilities as pet owners. Should Buster become too troublesome, however, the agreement allows us to return her to the humane society. But it takes only moments for a puppy to become a member of the family, so even if Buster had made toothpicks out of the end table, she would still have a home with us.

I have an even more secure place in the family of God. Though I try God's patience at times, he made a bargain that is far more binding than the one Tom and I made with the humane society. The terms of that agreement are outlined in John 3:16: "For God so lived the world that he gave his one and only Son, that whoever believes in him shall not perish but have eternal life." [1]

My friend Steve is skeptical about Christianity, that we can obtain salvation simply by believing that Jesus is the Savior, and that we can be so sure we'll never lose it. "So," he says, "what happens if I rob a bank and kill a bank guard? As long as I believe that Jesus is the Son of God and died to save my soul, I *still* go to heaven? Once saved always saved? No matter what?"

"Why do you ask?" I said. "Are you planning a bank heist and looking for 'heaven insurance'?"

It's more likely Steve is looking for excuses not to believe. In all probability neither he nor I will ever rob a bank. I, however, will at sometime in my life tell a lie—or two. If Christ had not already made provision for all of my sins, I'd have to wonder, *If I tell one lie a week can I still get into heaven? How about three lies a week? Or seven? Or a dozen?* God doesn't base my salvation on my behavior—he bases it on the payment Christ made for my sins and my acceptance of Christ's sacrifice.

When Tom and I chose Buster we were familiar with the basic nature of dogs, but we didn't know precisely what sort of personality Buster would have. Still, she never has to worry about how many pairs of loafers she can destroy before I pack her off to the humane society. God knew exactly what he was getting when he chose me, so I never have to worry that God will give up on me and throw me back.

Buster learns good behavior for a combination of reasons: she wants to avoid a scolding, she wants to please her humans, and she responds to conditioning. Once Buster is conditioned not to chew on certain things, she continues that behavior until she is taught otherwise.

I don't say that God trains me in the same way I train Buster, but once I made him the center of my life I did undergo a reconditioning of sorts. The Spirit of God in me produced a desire to be more Christlike rather than try to get away with as much as I can.

I'm glad that my ticket to heaven is not based on my behavior. But if I had the kind of attitude Steve expressed— a Christian can get away with murder and still get to heaven—I'd certainly hesitate to call myself a Christian.

For it is by grace you have been saved . . . not by works. . . . We are God's workmanship, created in Christ Jesus to do good works.
–Ephesians 2:8–10

If this is heaven, I want a futon.
--Buster the puppy

"You're living in dog heaven, you know that?" Dr. Leali said to Buster. Then he administered her last puppy shot. The veterinarian knew that Buster had been adopted from the humane society and that over the past couple of months she had gained weight and a sense of security. She had quickly adapted to the good food and tender affection she received in her paradise.

And neither was she shy about appropriating every available luxury. In our house, dogs are allowed on only one piece of furniture—the living room sofa (it's easy to clean). Everything else is off limits. We recently bought a futon for the screened-in porch, and after we assembled it we stood back to admire our work. Buster and Velvet ambled onto the porch to see what we were doing. Velvet sniffed at the futon, and I said to Tom, "Are we going to allow the dogs on—" Before I could finish the sentence Buster, without invitation or apology, hopped up and stretched out on the futon.

With my mouth still open I looked at Tom. He shrugged. It appeared that the dogs were allowed on a second piece of furniture. If this is heaven, then Buster needn't be satisfied with the bare necessities like food, water, and a dry place to sleep. Residents of heaven are entitled to toys, rides in the car, and the privilege of napping on a futon.

The word "entitled" is perhaps misapplied. Maybe deep down Buster thinks, *I'm one lucky pup!* Experts are divided on whether or not dogs feel gratitude, though some dogs appear to express gratitude under certain circumstances. It's certain, however, that dogs have no capacity for thankful thoughts like "I'm grateful that nothing bad happened today," or "I'm thankful to have been adopted by these nice people."

That's where dogs are different from people. If, like Buster, I'd been rescued from the brink of destruction and then had my every need taken care of, I'd be grateful every minute. I'd be satisfied with what I'd been given and never expect anything... um... more...and never...complain . . .

Right.

Come to think of it, dogs *are* different from people. Buster doesn't demand special treatment; she didn't ask for a futon to nap on. Nor does Buster feel she's privileged to live the good life. She merely accepts what is offered and feels neither entitled nor guilty. I, on the other hand, rejoice in and am thankful for the blessings God gives, but I sometimes want more and can't help but notice when I have less than my neighbors.

I may have questions about the blessings in this life, but the Bible says the system will be different in heaven. According to 1 Corinthians 3:8, "each will be rewarded according to his own labor." As a believer in Christ, my getting in the front gate of heaven is guaranteed. My goal, then, is to be such a good steward of my blessings that when I get to heaven I can expect more than being allowed to sleep on the floor at the foot of the bed.

The cynic might say that there's something wrong with doing good works just for rewards in heaven. But the cynic is missing the point. Once I had been touched by Christ, I wanted to become more Christlike. That means, in part, putting the needs of others before my own, extending hospitality, respecting my husband's leadership, sharing my blessings with others. I don't do good works for the rewards in heaven. I do good works *because* I'm going to heaven. Besides, the doing makes me feel good, and that's a pretty nice reward for the here and now.

Still, it's nice to know that when I get to heaven I will enter and then accept, as does Buster, without conceit or guilt, my futon.

Store up for yourselves treasures in heaven.
–Matthew 6:20

What's mine is mine!
~Velvet the dog

When Buster came to live with us she assumed everything in the house—including Velvet's toys—belonged to her. Velvet did not agree with Buster's assumption and in very clear terms let the puppy know that she was not welcome to share Velvet's possessions. Dogs like having their own things, and they do not understand the concepts of fairness and sharing.

When Buster picked up a rubber ring, Velvet streaked across the room, growled and snapped at the puppy, and took the ring away from her. Velvet lay down and kept the ring between her paws long enough to let Buster know that possession is nine-tenths of the law. Then after a few minutes she got up and left it. Buster waddled over to pick up the ring and the whole sequence started again.

Dr. Leali had advised us to let the dogs work out the terms of their own relationship, but I was often tempted to intervene. Instead, I mumbled while I watched events unfold: "Oh, Velvet! There are enough toys for both of you. Can't you share?"

I imagine God mumbles something similar when he sees us humans, who are so blessed with material possessions and yet reluctant to share. I used to think, *I work hard for everything I have. I earned this. I deserve it. Why should I give any of it away?*

The foremost reason is that God gave the ultimate gift—

his Son—to cancel the debt of my sins; and the greater the debt that is canceled, the greater should be the gratitude. The Bible gives me a number of other reasons as well: (1) "Whoever sows generously will also reap generously" (2 Cor. 9:6); (2) "Give to the one who asks you" (Matt. 5:42); (3) a person of noble character "opens her arms to the poor and extends her hands to the needy" (Prov. 31:20).

Those are all good reasons to share my blessings, but there's another consideration that motivates me. In Matthew 25:14-30, a master gave each of three servants some money, which they were to hold for him. Later, the master asked for an accounting—to see what each servant had done with the money he'd been given. The first two servants had invested their money and earned interest; the third had merely kept his hidden. The master was pleased with the first two servants and said, "Well done!" But the master was not pleased with the third servant, for he had only sat on his money.

Like Velvet's toys were given to her, so my possessions come ultimately from another source—God: "What do [I] have that [I] did not receive [from God]? (1 Cor. 4:7). And God did not provide his many blessings so I could keep them to myself. So when I stand before my Master and he asks for an accounting of what has been given to me, I want him to say, "Well done!"

Velvet's attitude is no longer, "What's mine is mine." This state of affairs has resulted not from Velvet's willingness to share. Buster has grown older and bigger, and it's just harder for Velvet to be stingy!

It's not hard, though, for me to be stingy. It's not hard to forget where my blessings come from. But one day I'll stand before God and he will ask, "What have you done with what

I gave you?" If I have to admit, "I didn't invest any of it for you,"—now that's going to be really hard!

*Let not your hand be open to receive
and clenched when it is time to give.*
–Sirach 4:31

I don't get no respect.
-General Custer the dog

My husband, Tom, loves to tell this story:

Years ago, Tom's neighbor Floyd was home alone one evening, watching his favorite television show. Floyd's old sheep dog, General Custer, had been napping but suddenly got up and paced the floor and whuffed and whined.

"Quiet down!" said Floyd. "I can't hear the TV when you're making all that racket."

Floyd propped his feet on the footstool and settled back in his chair, but General Custer paced and whuffed, growled and whined. Floyd got irritated and yelled, "Go lay down and be quiet, you nutty dog!"

The old dog gazed at Floyd, then padded to his favorite rug. He circled a few times, then plopped down and heaved a sigh.

The next day when Floyd went to the garage, the side door hung open. All the hubcaps had been stolen from his car! General Custer hadn't been crazy after all. He'd sensed something was wrong and tried to alert Floyd.

In the Old Testament, several different prophets tried to alert the kingdoms of Judah and Israel of impending trouble. Some of those prophets seemed more than a little crazy. Ezekiel, for instance, shaved off his beard and his hair with a sword; for 390 days he laid down on his left side, then for 40 days on his right side. Another prophet, Jeremiah, acted out little plays and for a time carried a heavy yoke.

The prophets of the kingdoms of Israel and Judah tried to warn the populace that they would suffer God's punishment if they didn't change their immoral behaviors. And that sounded crazy, too. Both kingdoms had ignored God's laws for a long time and had prospered through their immorality. Their religious leaders assured them they had nothing to fear. Then along came those absurd prophets who claimed to speak for God. Neither kingdom listened to the prophets, and the people paid for their disobedience.

In a nearby suburb lives a man named Mr. Burns. He paints Bible verses all over the exterior of his house. While driving on the highway, I sometimes see cars or vans plastered side and back with bumper stickers, all of them bearing Bible verses and religious sayings. I happened to drive past a residence where a family was collecting food to aid the hungry. The yard was full of placards that read "Jesus saves"; "For God so loved the world . . ."; "the wages of sin is death," and so forth. Gospel music blared from a loud speaker.

Mr. Burns, the bumper-stickered drivers, the charitable people with the yard full of placards—they all remind me a little of Old Testament prophets: They appear to be eccentric, but they're trying to deliver a message.

On a recent episode of the television program, *Touched by an Angel*, one of the characters, a baker, claimed to have seen the devil. Everyone thought the baker was "traumatized" after witnessing a brutal crime. An angel, though, told the baker that he wasn't crazy—that he was a prophet of God. The angel said something like, "Prophets don't have psychic powers and they don't tell the future from their own instinct. God uses a prophet to tell the truth and to shine a light in the darkness."

Tell the truth—that's what Ezekiel and Jeremiah and the other Old Testament prophets tried to do. Shine the light of God's truth—that's what individuals like Mr. Burns try to do with their painted signs and their placards.

Floyd ignored General Custer and dismissed his whuffing and whining as the ramblings of a restless old dog. It's easy to dismiss the Mr. Burnses of this world as crackpots and fanatics, but dismissing their message could end in far greater loss than a few hubcaps.

The wise will be put to shame; . . . Since they have rejected the word of the Lord, what kind of wisdom do they have?
—Jeremiah 8:9

Chipmunks have a real attitude.
~Velvet the dog

A chipmunk is about the size of a dog's tongue. Nonetheless, the sound a chipmunk makes is called a bark. To be more precise, a sassy bark. Experts say that animals behave according to instinct and the laws of survival. Probably so, but the instinctive behavior of some animals appears to be plain old impudence. And in some cases, it appears that the smaller the creature the greater the impudence.

Consider the aforementioned chipmunk. We have oak trees around our house, which means we also have acorns, which means we have squirrels and chipmunks. Squirrels amuse themselves by dangling upside down in the trees and flipping the bowl off the birdbath. Chipmunks amuse themselves by provoking Velvet and Buster. One chipmunk in particular—I call him Pockets—has a real attitude.

Last fall Pockets used the fenced-in portion of our yard as a short cut for gathering acorns, and the chain-link fence gave him an opportunity to play tag with Velvet and Buster. He slipped through the fence on one side of the house and scurried across the yard. When he was about twenty feet from the fence on the other side of the house, Velvet noticed him and launched into pursuit. Pockets evaluated the situation, adjusted his speed accordingly, and zipped through the fence just in the nick of time.

Not content, however, with his narrow escape, Pockets

had to rub in the fact that he'd bested Velvet. He hopped up on a stump that sits about six feet outside the fence, and barked—chip, chip, chip. Velvet pressed her nose against the fence—WOOF, WOOF, WOOF. I heard the exchange through the kitchen window—WOOF, CHIP, WOOF, CHIP.

"You little rascal," I said to Pockets. "If it weren't for the fence, you wouldn't be so brave."

That scenario got me to thinking about people who seem to get away with risking their own well-being. After the Israelites settled in Canaan they lived a pretty good life. Then they did something foolhardy—they turned to idol worship. God had warned them that idol worship would get them into trouble. Not only did idol worship insult God, it led to other foolish behavior, like cheating one another out of goods and property, and indulging in sexual promiscuity.

Prophets of God nipped at the heels of the Israelites—as Velvet nipped at the heels of Pockets—warning them about the consequences of their behavior. But the Israelites said, "We've gotten away with it so far and nothing bad has happened to us." The Israelites thought they were immune from danger, and they were, in fact, protected by a barrier, one more effective than a chain-link fence—God's patience and long-suffering. That barrier, though, eventually eroded and the Israelites were punished severely.

When I read that account in the Bible I think, *How could the Israelites have been so foolish?* But then I remember the last time I raced through a yellow traffic light and wonder, *How could I have been so foolish?* Simple. We take foolish risks because we think we can get away with it.

Whether it's running yellow lights or cheating on one's spouse, if it's accomplished without adverse consequences, the transgressor becomes complacent: "I've gotten away with it so far and nothing bad has happened to me." That attitude, however, is flawed. First, it conveys the idea that one behaves morally only out of fear of consequences rather than because of upright character. Second, it suggests that immoral behavior is no big deal as long as "no one is hurt."

Excuse me! If no one has yet suffered it's not because the behavior isn't risky. It's because God is patient.

And God is certainly more patient than I. Sometimes it seems as if everybody is getting away with something. I feel like Velvet must feel when she woofs at Pockets from inside the fence. She'd like the barrier to come down and the scoffer to get what-for.

As for Pockets, he's still taking foolish risks and getting away with it. But because chipmunks have no sense of morality, he doesn't know there is such a thing as consequences. So Pockets grows sleek on acorns and scoots under Velvet's nose with his tail straight up; he barks his sassy bark and feels safe because he's gotten away with it so far and nothing bad has happened.

Well, I offer Pockets a note of caution: remember the Israelites.

We may never be able to tempt God beyond the point that he is able to protect us, but we may certainly tempt him beyond that which he is willing to protect us.
—Michael Hodgin

I need a pack leader.
–Buster the puppy

"Give your dog the command to sit," said Mike, the trainer. He was talking to the tall woman with the tiny dog. It was the second class of obedience training, and we were standing in a circle while Mike worked with Pancho, a recalcitrant Chihuahua. At the word "sit" all of our dogs simultaneously plopped down.

We all laughed, and Mike said, "This is a good object lesson. When you're training your dog, use a confident tone, as if you expected to be obeyed. A dog recognizes a voice with authority."

Most of us in the class lacked that kind of authority. On the first day we'd learned that the hardest part of training a dog is training the owner. Dogs willingly do what is asked of them, but the owners must first be taught how to ask. The humans in our class were still struggling: we said "stop it," or "don't" when we meant "no!" Some of us kept the dogs' leads too long, others kept them too short; we forgot to make eye contact with our dogs when giving commands. We didn't watch our dogs while we paraded them in a circle (which could be untidy if the collie ahead of you had to make a pit stop).

But as the weeks passed, we humans gained confidence and the dogs' performances improved in direct proportion. (Pancho remained recalcitrant.) But at home my obedience-school demeanor slipped. If Buster pestered me for attention I'd mumble, "Stop it . . . don't." Then I'd come to myself, look Buster in the eye, and say in a kind but firm tone, "No. Down," and Buster would go lie down. I'm still amazed when that works. I shouldn't be, though. Wild canine packs are arranged in a hierarchy, and the pack needs an alpha dog, a "top dog" if you will, to keep order. The entire pack is more content and self-confident with a strong alpha dog. A domesticated dog perceives its human as the alpha dog.

Because of my experience working with Buster at obedience school, I better understand the stir Jesus created when he taught in the synagogues. The book of Matthew tells how the crowds listened to Jesus because he spoke with authority, and now I have a better idea of what speaking with authority means.

I once heard authority described as "legitimized power," that is, authority backed up by credentials. Mike, for instance, has credentials: thirty years of training dogs and an AKC certification. So when he begins a training session, Mike is confident he can handle any situation. Dogs sense Mike's self-confidence and they feel secure that this man is worthy of their trust and their obedience.

Jesus had prime credentials. He spoke with authority because of the power that was behind that authority—God— a Power who was intimately acquainted with all sides of human nature, who knew the heart of each person in an audience and what would touch each one. No wonder Jesus convinced so many doubtful listeners to seek the kingdom of God. When Jesus taught, his listeners felt secure that this man was worthy of their trust and allegiance.

That day at obedience school when Mike commanded Pancho to "sit" and every dog obeyed, we all laughed. Our dogs recognized that Mike spoke with authority, and soon Buster responded to me as eagerly as she had to Mike. A human, too, obeys more than one master: parents, government, (dare I say?) spouse. But there is one Master whose voice carries more authority than all the others, and His words are the teaching that truly counts.

When Jesus had finished saying these things, the crowds were amazed at his teaching, because he taught as one who had authority.
–Matthew 7:28–29

I'm not Lassie—keep it simple.
–Buster the puppy

"Buster, sit!" I commanded. Buster grinned at me and wagged her tail.

Hmm.

I placed one hand on Buster's rump and gently but firmly pushed down. "Buster, sit!" After being pushed down and given the "sit" command several times, Buster sat on command without me touching her.

"Good gir-r-r-l!"

It was clear that Buster enjoyed the dog obedience class sponsored by the humane society. The training stimulated her mind, exercised her body, and earned her prodigious amounts of praise and attention.

"We start with something simple and then build on it," said Mike, the trainer. "First we'll teach the 'sit' command and then progress to the 'stay' and 'down' commands."

The class would last for eight weeks, but in the first two weeks alone, Buster went from an undisciplined dog to a more confident dog who responded to three separate commands: sit, stay, and come. Cool! The humane society stressed patience, praise, and practice as well as taking things one step at a time.

One step at a time. That's the way God leads me along this walk we call Christian life. To live godly, one must accept much that runs against the grain of human nature, like yielding complete leadership to God and placing the concerns of others before those of oneself. A few years ago I was ready for only the first simple step—accepting the fact that God loved me. That first simple step led me to the second—recommitting to my faith in God.

The relief and satisfaction I felt as a result was a gift from God. I did nothing to merit that gift, but I accepted it without hesitation. And that led to the next step—understanding that gift as the grace of God. Over the past few years I've matured in faith, and in gratitude for God's grace I've tried to walk a more godly path. Most of my steps have been very small, but one or two have taken me a long way indeed.

For years I had a bad habit. I tore at the cuticles on my fingers until they bled. My fingers were so sore that the throbbing sometimes awakened me in the middle of the night. I felt as if the habit were a demon I couldn't exorcise. So I prayed for healing.

Over an eighteen-month period I embarked on three different prayer campaigns. During the first campaign my motive was misguided; I wanted pretty hands. I restrained the habit for a week or so, and then I was back to sore fingers. During the second campaign I didn't care about pretty hands, I just wanted my fingers to stop being sore. "Lord," I prayed, "I can't break this terrible habit alone. I need your help." The results were the same as the first time.

Then one night I read in the Bible about Gideon. His army was small in number and faced a mighty foe, but before the battle, Gideon exhorted his soldiers not to be afraid: "The Lord has given the [enemy] into your hands" (Judg. 7:15). Gideon spoke as if the victory was already accomplished, because that's how God had presented it to him.

It occurred to me, *That's the kind of thinking it takes to prevail against my bad habit.* God was powerful enough to effect a victory without Gideon's help, and he is powerful enough to effect my healing without my help. In a way I can't explain, I realized that all I needed to do was accept the healing.

The prayer for my third campaign was, "Father, I know that you want me to be healed and that you have the power to heal me. I know that in your eyes my healing has already taken place, so thank you, Father, for healing me. In Jesus' name, amen."

One evening a few nights into the campaign, I felt particularly fidgety and nibbled at a finger. I felt, rather than heard, "Do you think I cannot do this for you?" From that night onward I felt confident I would be healed. If God wants something to be accomplished, what can stop it? As I write this my hands look, if not pretty, at least normal, and I'm no longer awakened by throbbing fingers.

I don't blame you if you're thinking, *Oh, please!* A few years ago I, too, expressed doubt when I heard stories like this. And truth be told, when I started the third prayer campaign I neither believed nor disbelieved the content of my prayer. But the more I repeated the prayer the more believable it sounded.

Understanding Christianity is as simple as saying, "I love Jesus," and as complex as the nature of the Trinity. So God meets me where I am, starting with the first simple steps and building on them. Though my healing is not an indication of special standing in the eyes of God, that I was able to *accept* healing does indicate that I am maturing in my faith. I may never fully understand how something can be accomplished before it happens; I only know that, in this instance, it is true.

Buster is a relatively simple creature and, once she

understands what I want, is eager to please me. Compared to God, I'm a pathetically simple creature and it's going to take me awhile to understand some of the nuances of his teaching. So please, God, when you're instructing me, remember: I'm not Lassie. Keep it simple.

The Holy Spirit has not reached the end of what He has to tell us.
-Arthur John Gossip

Obedience school is not about cute tricks.
~Buster the puppy

"Leave it" is a valuable command. It means "keep your mouth off," and when Buster examines a piece of road kill, that command alone is worth every penny I paid for obedience school! Obedience training has additional practical purposes for both Buster and me.

• Training gave me enough confidence to let Buster know I'm the boss, and once Buster yielded to my authority she felt more secure, knowing who is in charge.

• Training reinforced the bond between Buster and me. Training requires that I make eye contact with her, and she enjoys having my full attention. She also loves the praise she gets when she obeys commands.

• Training helped Buster learn self-restraint, which makes her much easier to live with.

• Training taught Buster useful commands, like "leave it," that are not just for my sake. "Leave it" keeps Buster from destroying things or from eating something that could make her ill.

• Training encouraged Buster to walk politely on a leash without pulling. Therefore I'm able to take her for walks and give her exercise.

By the end of the eight-week course, Buster learned several basic commands and how to walk on a leash; she grew less excitable, more confident, and developed self-control. Obedience training does not teach impractical tricks like sit up and beg, roll over and play dead, or any other cute stuff.

(Buster is already cuter than any dog has a right to be.) Training doesn't require that she be anything other than a dog. It merely helps her become a well-behaved and a happier dog.

Obedience to God yields practical results, too. Mike, my and Buster's trainer, once told the class about Butch, a troublesome German shepherd who wouldn't yield to authority. Butch's behavior bears a resemblance to my old self: he wouldn't get out of a car (I was rebellious), he barked and lunged at other dogs (I was irritable), and he had to be isolated from other dogs (I sulked when things didn't go my way). I bristled at the very suggestion of obeying. I envisaged obedience as God making me jump hurdles and forbidding me to have any fun. Besides, people who bowed their heads and murmured "it is God's will" struck me as naive.

Clearly, I did not understand the purpose for obedience, and rather than bend to "God's will," I rebelled: "I'm in control of my life, and I'll make things happen my way." For instance, I once took a clerical job that seemed perfect for me. I was trying to get my own business going at that time, and the clerical work was part time and did not tax my skills and energy. After a couple of months on the job I realized I'd made a mistake. I got irritable, I pouted, and then I quit.

I read that one of the purposes for yielding to God's leadership is so he can accomplish great things through those who are yielded to him. I guess I'm still waiting for the "great thing," but when I pray for guidance and wait to see where God will lead—rather than trying to make things happen—I do see results. My life is less complicated and less stressful, and events often occur in fortuitous order, as if they have been planned.

Some people might say that now I'm the one who's being naive. But God has existed forever, and his teaching reflects an infinity of wisdom. Yielding to greater wisdom is prudent; it is not blind obedience.

Obedience training helped Butch, the troublesome German shepherd, become affectionate and contented. Before I yielded to the greater wisdom of God, I, like Butch, was defiant and often angry. Then I realized that the purpose for obedience is not so God can put me through an obstacle course. Obedience allows God to guide me through the obstacles in life.

Blessed is [he] who . . . rejoices that he received instruction from the Lord.
–C. H. Spurgeon

I found out that obedience is not a dirty word.
~Velvet the dog

"Velvet, sit. . . . Velvet, sit. . . . Velvet, SIT!" It was not going well.

Because Buster was responding nicely to obedience training, I thought I'd use the training techniques on Velvet. Velvet has been generally well-behaved and almost trouble-free from the first day I brought her home, but she's not always compliant. She often does not respond immediately when called, and she pulls on the leash when we take a walk.

I thought Velvet would enjoy the training sessions. When I worked with Buster in the yard, Velvet raced from window to window, watching and whining as if consumed by jealousy. So after I worked with Buster and put her in the house, I snapped the lead on Velvet and led her out into the yard. She immediately dug in her heels. She had to be pressed into the sit position every time, and pressed into the down position. Nor did she want to walk a figure eight around the chairs I'd set up. She was rebellious and appeared to be offended: "I've been a perfectly delightful dog for six years, Paulette, and now you're making me do this dumb stuff."

I explained the situation to Mike. "It's my own fault," I said. "Velvet's never had any obedience training. She's never had to do anything except exist."

"It's not too late," he said. "But it will take longer to train Velvet. Just be patient and consistent and she'll come around."

I worked with Velvet almost every day but made little progress, and I was growing frustrated. *Maybe I'll just live with her the way she is*, I thought. But I knew that in order to win Velvet's respect, she must recognize that I am in charge. After a few weeks Velvet obeyed commands but resisted looking me in the eye. Her attitude was, "I'll do it, but this is insulting." So much for teaching an old dog new tricks.

I could empathize with her; my own attitude toward obedience was rebellious. In the first place, there are precious few individuals who merit obedience or can be trusted not to exploit it. Besides, obedience seemed like such an old-fashioned and repressive concept. The very word left a bad taste in my mouth.

It's human nature to resist authority, and it was particularly hard for me to admit I needed to obey God. But God's character and his qualifications to command are far different from those of humans. God created everything, and he sustains everything. All that I presently have or am comes ultimately from God, and he has even secured my future in heaven. God never has ulterior or selfish motives for requiring obedience, nor would he demand I do anything destructive to myself or others.

That's not to say that obedience is always easy. Sometimes I don't feel like putting the needs of others before my own, and I'm often disappointed when God's plans aren't the same as mine. Plus, it's often just plain hard to do what is right.

Although I wanted to obey God, the word *obedience* stuck in my craw. In my reading, I'd seen obedience defined in different ways: following God's direction, or yielding to God's wisdom. Those terms sounded more user-friendly than *obey*.

Since I knew obedience was a struggle for me, I prayed about it. At first my prayer was, "Dear God, help me to follow your direction." When I got used to the sound of that, my prayer became, "Lord, help me to yield to your wisdom." Now I am able to use the O word when I pray: "Father, help me to obey." I laugh now at how I resisted using the word obey, but using it was a milestone in my faith.

Like Velvet, I'd spent most of my life living the way I wanted to, and it was hard for both of us to yield to authority. Though Velvet still does not cheerfully respond to commands, she seems more secure in knowing that someone has at last taken charge. Neither do I always obey with a cheerful heart. But, knowing that God is worthy of obedience and is qualified to command, I remind myself, *God knows what he's doing. Trust him.*

The child wants more indulgence; the father expects more obedience.
                                    –Oliver Goldsmith (paraphrased)

I love to chase and carry; I don't like to let go.
~Velvet the dog

"Velvet, leave it," I commanded. Velvet tugged on the Frisbee, and her eyes shone as she gurgled a benign growl.

"Leave it," I repeated. Velvet tugged. "Leave it!"

The trainer said that in a battle of wills with a dog, the owner must win so the dog will understand who's the boss. So I tried prying Velvet's mouth open with my fingers. "L-e-e-e-v IT!" Her jaws were like a steel trap.

"Forget it," I said. "I'm not going to play with you anymore." I turned to go into the house, and when my hand touched the doorknob, Velvet dropped the Frisbee. I snatched it up. "Good gir-r-r-l!" I had won, but by default.

I explained my problem to Mike. "Velvet loves to run after a toy and she carries it right back to me, but she won't let it go. You'd think she'd put two and two together. I can't throw the toy if she won't let go."

"Well," said Mike, "for a dog, chasing and retrieving are instinctive. Letting go is not."

Humans, too, behave in a similar way. We chase after a dream, for instance, carry it around with us, and even when the dream is clearly beyond reach, we are loath to let it go.

I teach a creative writing workshop to seniors. One of the writers, a woman in her seventies named Gladys, read her story about pursuing a dream and having to let it go.

"When my husband, Henry, and I were first married," she read, "we dreamed about having children—two boys and two girls. We wondered who our children would look

like—my side of the family or Henry's. We talked about taking the children camping and going on picnics, and we even
talked about starting a college fund.

"We tried to have a baby for seven years, but each month
we were disappointed. That was long before fertility drugs
and test-tube babies, you know. We just had to let nature
take its course."

Eventually, Gladys was told by her doctor that there was
no possibility she would ever bear a child. After years of pursuing their dream and carrying it in their hearts, Gladys and
Henry had to relinquish it. But Gladys, especially, had difficulty letting go.

"I was so angry at God," Gladys continued, "because I
would never carry a baby inside me or nurse a baby at my
breast."

Henry suggested they adopt, but she resisted the idea.

"I was stubborn," she wrote. "I wanted to see my mother's eyes looking at me from my daughter's face and hear my
father's laughter coming from my son's throat."

While visiting her cousin Millie, Gladys met a young
mother with a toddler. "I felt my heart break as I looked into
the child's face," Gladys read. "'Your daughter looks a lot
like you,'" I said to the young mother, and she beamed with
pride. After the mother and child left, Millie said to me, "
'Gladys, that child is adopted.'

"That day marked the beginning of a change in me,
because that day my spirit began to heal."

Gladys and Henry adopted a daughter, then a son, and
then another daughter. It's true that long ago more babies
were available for adoption, but even so, it was unusual for
one couple to be given three babies. It appeared to be God's

purpose that Gladys and her husband share their lives with those particular children.

Gladys thinks so, too. And she is filled with a sense of that purpose through the love she shares with her children, her grandchildren—and her brand new great granddaughter.

I still struggle with Velvet over the Frisbee. But if I turn my back to her and pretend I'm not interested, she usually drops it. Gladys struggled, too, to hold on to a hopeless dream. But God did not turn his back on Gladys.

One joy was expected and another is given. . . turn from the good expected to the given good.
–C.S. Lewis

Listen to my bark and get a clue.
-Velvet the dog

Velvet is more territorial than Buster. Velvet barks when another dog comes near the yard; Buster heads for the house. Velvet barks when an unfamiliar person approaches the fence; Buster wags and grins. Actually, Buster doesn't bark much at all, but Velvet barks enough for both of them.

A dog's bark transmits information. In the wild, canines bark to keep other creatures out of their territory and to alert the pack to danger. Pack members bark at one another for reassurance. Velvet's barking accomplishes much the same thing: it sounds a warning to anyone who may be approaching, and it alerts me when something is going on. It reassures me of her vigilance, as my vocal response reassures her that the pack leader has been alerted.

The type of bark Velvet uses—her "tone of voice"—gives me a clue in deciphering her message.

Woo-woo-woo-woo-woo means, "Someone is jogging by out in the street." That same sound, but approaching hysteria, means, "There's a dog on the other side of the fence!"

Wuh-wuh-WHOOOOOOO-wuh-wuh-WOOOOOOO delivered in a screeching yodel means a person is approaching the house.

Whuff . . . Whuff . . . tossed here and there while she's pacing in the house or yard means, "I'm on duty."

God uses different tones of voice, too. I've never heard an audible message from heaven, but I'm convinced God uses various means to communicate with me.

- While driving one frosty morning I didn't realize there were thin patches on the street, and I skidded through an intersection. Fortunately, no cars were coming, and I immediately adjusted my speed for conditions. Message received.
- I struggled and prayed before making a difficult decision, and I wondered if I'd made the right choice. The same day a radio talk-show host said, "If a decision you've made was hard and a little scary, you've probably made the right decision." Message received.
- During a period when I became discouraged while writing this book, I had dreams about following dog tracks, about rescuing a drowning dog, and about finding a lost dog—all themes about not giving up on the dog. Message received.

A skeptic might say that I'm sifting an ordinary event—like a dream—through whatever happens to be on my mind, and am merely interpreting that event—the dream—as a message.

Could be. But I look at it this way: If I didn't know much about dogs, I wouldn't know that dogs keep watch and that a dog's bark provides information. So I wouldn't pay much attention to barking. But I *do* know that dogs keep watch, and that Velvet barks for a reason. Therefore, it would be imprudent to ignore her barking.

In a similar way, if I didn't believe in God—or that God took an active interest in my life—I wouldn't be expecting any messages, so I wouldn't be listening for them. But I *do* believe that God is concerned about me and that he *does* communicate with me. And that it is very prudent, indeed, to heed his messages.

There are days when Velvet barks every few minutes, but since I can tell by her tone that she just sees a jogger I can safely ignore her. I can't imagine a scenario in which it would be wise to ignore a message from God. Trouble is, I haven't yet learned all of his tones of voice, nor do I listen often enough to those still, small voices. So while I heed the messages I receive, I can't help but wonder how many never get through!

He made thee to hear his voice, that he might instruct thee.
--Deuteronomy 4:36 (KJV)

When I can't look any cuter, I do something adorable.
                                        -Buster the puppy

Buster was lying on her side next to my chair. One ear flopped over an eye and her head rested on one paw. "Could you possibly look any cuter?" I said to her. She stretched full length, tucked her head between her front paws, and squinted her eyes. Her response, it seems, was, "Yes, I can. How's this?" In response to her, I scratched her tummy.

It wasn't enough for Buster that she merely look cute; she had to do something adorable. She doesn't realize, of course, that she's cute. And she doesn't know looking cute prompts me to scratch her tummy. People, though, are different. Attractive people are usually aware of their own appearance, and a measure of maturity is how a person feels about her or his own good looks. One person thinks, *I'm gorgeous and that makes me special.* Another thinks, *My good looks are not something I earned; it's a genetic fluke and I'm no more special than anyone else.*

The second attitude might reflect the way Esther, the biblical beauty, felt about her appearance. Esther's beauty was more than skin deep, and rather than merely sit back and reap the rewards of her good fortune, she did something that demonstrated her beautiful character.

Esther was a Jew who lived in the Persian Empire and, because of her beauty, was chosen by King Xerxes to be his queen. Haman, a man of high standing in the king's court, hated the Jews and conspired to have them destroyed. When Esther's cousin, Mordecai, discovered the plot, he urged

Esther to speak with the king to save her people. Esther was fearful, because to approach the king unsummoned was a capital offense. Though she hesitated at first, Esther recognized her duty and was successful in persuading the king to spare the Jews.

God had blessed Esther with great beauty, then placed her in a position of influence, thereby affecting the course of events. God also made Buster cute, and her cuteness influences me—to scratch her tummy. The analogy seems like a stretch, but God created all living creatures and he endows each with special gifts. And that's where the comparison ends.

Buster doesn't know she has a pleasing appearance and she doesn't know her appearance influences human behavior, whereas Esther was aware of her beauty and the influence it had on Xerxes. And although dogs have personalities and a certain kind of nature, they do not develop character—in the sense of making a decision to behave admirably. Esther, on the other hand, made a conscious decision to act with courage, and she used her beauty as a blessing, to achieve an admirable rather than a selfish purpose.

We are all blessed in some way with a gift from God, and how we use that gift tells a lot about us. I like to write about my dogs and how their behavior reminds me, in a wacky way, about my relationship with God. When I consider Buster's cuteness—a God-given characteristic—it reminds me of Esther's beauty—a God-given characteristic. And every time my dogs do something adorable I realize that God gives all his creatures some special blessing, and I'm thereby reminded that God is my best friend.

God hides his Glory in the oddest places.
–Eugene Peterson

• ETERNITY •

I never tire of having my tummy scratched.
–Velvet the dog

Dogs are easy to please. Toss a stick and a dog will bound after it in ecstasies of joy. Thirty tosses later, the dog is still bounding as if stick tossing were the most novel game ever devised. Not only are dogs easy to please, they never tire of something they enjoy. Take a tummy scratch, for instance.

When I sit on the couch and watch *Jeopardy!* Velvet usually sits next to me. I stroke her back while I concentrate on beating the contestants to the answer . . . uh . . . question: "Who is Winslow Homer?!"

In the meantime, Velvet executes a subtle maneuver. While lying on her tummy, she casually leans toward me and rolls onto her side. Then, inch by inch, she slides onto her back. At the first commercial break I notice that I'm now scratching Velvet's tummy. Twenty minutes later at the conclusion of Final Jeopardy, Velvet has not moved another muscle and I'm still scratching her tummy. I have no idea how long she would lie in one position and have her tummy scratched, but my fingers would probably cramp up long before she became disenchanted.

I even joked about it once: "I bet Velvet could spend eternity having her tummy scratched."

That joke made me wonder, *What would keep me contented for eternity?* I sometimes think about heaven—what it will be like and how I will be occupied. So I took a cue from Velvet and asked myself, "What are some things that I never tire of?"

I never tire of watching the seasons change. Even if I live

to be a hundred, I'll experience the colors of autumn only one hundred times. That doesn't seem nearly enough.

I never tire of the scent of flowers. In the spring I open the bedroom windows at night and inhale the aroma of lilies-of-the-valley while I lie in bed. The blossoms fade after only a couple of weeks, far too quickly for me to get my fill, and I can't imagine ever growing weary of their fragrance.

I never tire of hearing the wind blowing through the pine trees. We have three or four varieties of pines around our house, most of them planted sixty years ago by the Civilian Conservation Corps. The tallest ones reach high above the roof of the house and whisper with every breeze.

I never tire of stroking Buster's silky brown ears or Velvet's soft black cheeks.

The idea of existing for eternity is incomprehensible and almost frightening. Having time without end is so alien to the way I experience life. And what would consume my time—forever? Many writers have speculated about heaven. Some say we will have no concept of time as we know it now. Others say we will have important work to do in the next life.

I just have to trust God, that he has everything worked out and that he knows what his children need. I hope, though, the new heaven and the new earth has flowers and changes of seasons, pine forests and pets. Because there are things in the here and now I can't get enough of. And if, as some of the writers say, what I experience today is but a shadow of what is yet to come, then what glorious seasons, what intoxicating scents, bewitching sounds, and enticing textures I can experience to my heart's content—forever!

When our expectations are given over to [God],
we have nothing to fear and everything to anticipate.
–Robert J. Radcliffe

• GOD'S CARE •

To know me is to love me.
–Buster the puppy

It takes about five seconds to fall in love with a puppy. When we first met Buster at the humane society, she appeared so lost and abandoned that my heart went out to her. After she'd lived with us a few days, the regular meals and worm medication produced an overall improvement in Buster's condition. As a result of her increased energy she squirmed and chewed when I held her, tugged at my pant legs, and dragged my shoes around the living room. What's not to love?

The longer Buster lived with us, the more she endeared herself to me, and I've come to appreciate her little quirks. She lies at my feet while I work, peeks in the window when she wants to come in, crowds out Velvet for the spot next to me on the couch.

I was first drawn to Buster because puppies have an obvious attribute—they're adorable. But I grew to love Buster because of the little things that make up her unique personality. I've grown to love God through a similar process. Yes, I first loved God because he loved me first and sacrificed his Son for my sins. And beyond that I was amazed by his obvious attributes that are displayed through creation.

Recently Tom and I visited the local botanical gardens. Birds have been introduced into the conservatory, and on the day we visited, a covey of Chinese quail darted in and out amid the ground cover. A baby quail is about the size of a bumblebee and has a heart not much larger than a sesame seed. My husband bent low and peered at a string of chicks scurrying after their mother, then he turned to me and said, "And some people don't believe in God."

Such a being is God that he possesses the subtlety to create a delicate baby quail . . . and the power to create a sun. What's not to love?

Amazed as I am by the attributes of God evident in creation, I am awed by God's attention to the details of my life.

I have sinus problems, and sometimes my whole face aches. I take allergy medications, and my doctor advises against combining them with over-the-counter sinus pills. After enduring sinus pain for several days in a row I prayed, "Father, I know there are millions people who are suffering with terrible diseases. I'm not asking you to cure my sinuses, but help me to cope with this aching in my face."

The next morning at breakfast my husband said, "Why don't you call your allergist and see if he can suggest anything?" I called, and the nurse told me to take ibuprofen for the inflammation and to inhale steam to loosen the congestion. A few drops of eucalyptus oil in the hot water would help clear my lungs. I tried it and felt much better. God didn't cure my sinus problems, but he provided the means, through my husband and a concerned nurse, for me to get relief.

When I first saw Buster I was touched by her obvious charms, and as I got to know her, I grew to love her even more. When I consider the splendor of God, so obvious in everything from the delicacy of a baby quail to the power of the sun, I am amazed. And when I consider what God sacrificed for my redemption, I am humbled. But the more I know of God, the more I consider how he attends to even the smallest concerns in my life.

As for the sinus-prayer experience, that sort of thing doesn't happen often, but when it does I feel that I have encountered all-encompassing love. And I am awed.

Be still and know that I am God.
—Psalm 46:10

It may be a filthy stuffed bear, but it's my filthy stuffed bear.
~Velvet the dog

Velvet and Buster share all the toys, but there is one exception—the bear. Ownership of that particular toy is nonnegotiable. It belongs to Velvet. The bear is about eight inches tall and was, when I first brought it home a few weeks ago, white.

I bought the bear at a fund-raiser for leukemia organized by Bill, a young tennis pro who underwent a bone marrow transplant. When Bill's hair fell out he wore a do-rag, and Bill and his do-rag have now come to symbolize a local organization that promotes bone marrow donations. The little bears sold at the fund-raiser each wore a black bow tie and a calico do-rag.

When I brought the bear home I laid it on the kitchen table while I put away some groceries. The next time I looked, Velvet—*Velvet!*—had her front paws on one of the chairs and, ever-so-carefully, took the bear's foot between just her front teeth and slid it . . . off . . . the table. Then she trotted off to the living room.

It's uncharacteristic of Velvet to help herself that way, and I stood there with my mouth hanging open. I followed her into the living room, where she was curled up on the sofa—resting her chin on the bear.

Over the next few weeks, Velvet and Buster tussled over the bear. They quickly shredded the bow tie and the do-rag, and the bear turned gray. But it remained Velvet's special possession. Buster could tug on it but could not take it away from her. If Velvet came in from outside and Buster had the bear, Buster was immediately dispossessed of it.

When the toy's soiled condition became truly unpleasant to live with, I tossed it on top of a garbage bag full of trash in the garage. Later that day when I looked up from pruning, Velvet was carrying the bear. She had followed me into the garage when I'd gotten the yard tools. "Velvet," I shouted, "put down that filthy bear!" Velvet's head snapped up and she looked at me, the bear still dangling from her mouth. Her expression said it all, "It may be a filthy stuffed bear, but it's *my* filthy stuffed bear."

She was determined to hold on to that toy no matter how ugly it had become. I was reminded of a scene from C.S. Lewis's *The Great Divorce*, a fanciful tale that takes place in heaven. Shining spirit-beings try to convince the newly arrived and translucent ghosts to divorce themselves from their corrupt attitudes, which make the ghosts too insubstantial to exist in paradise. One ghost carried on his shoulder a small, evil-looking red lizard, which represented the ghost's lewd habits. A shining spirit offered to destroy the lizard, and the ghost wanted to be rid of the horrid creature but couldn't quite bring himself to relinquish it. At last the ghost broke down and cried out to the spirit, "Go on . . . get it over!" From the remains of the dead lizard a beautiful white stallion with a golden mane was resurrected. The ghost, who had himself begun to shine, hopped astride the steed and rode at a gallop toward paradise.

For decades, I too carried around my own nasty beast—a nervous habit that left my fingers looking wounded and ugly. I wanted to be free of the beast, but at every attempt I failed to relinquish it. When I finally let God destroy the habit, no magical creature arose from its remains, nor did I expect any such thing. What did result was a fuller understanding of what can be accomplished through surrendering to God's caring.

Velvet's filthy stuffed bear has since gone on to that great hibernation in the sky. After one too many games of tug-of-war the bear degenerated into a pile of shredded gray matter. I, too, witnessed the demise of a beast that I had long been unable to release. As a result of its death I was not transported to paradise, but I have experienced a kind of freedom—I am less encumbered for the next step to where God is leading me.

My power is made perfect in weakness.
-2 Corinthians 12:9

I do my job better when someone is watching.
–Spike the dog

"That dog irritates me!" Tom had just come in from taking Velvet for a walk, and he grumbled while he took off his shoes.

"Why?" I said. "What did she do?"

"Not Velvet," he said. "That O.L.D. at the end of the cul-de-sac."

"O.L.D.?"

"Obnoxious little dog."

"Oh," I said. "You mean Spike."

Spike is a short—but husky—brown dog of mixed heritage, and he is very territorial. His owners installed an invisible fence, but when someone walks by his house, Spike scrabbles down the driveway, barking every inch of the way to the very edge of his boundary.

"His owners were out on the front steps tonight," Tom said, "so he was even more obnoxious than usual. He kept looking over his shoulder to see if they were watching him do his stuff."

Spike reminds me of the hypocrites in the New Testament—those respected members of the religious establishment—whom Jesus rebuked for their shallow piety. Spike valued his owners' approval, so when they were watching he barked with uninhibited enthusiasm and charged along his boundary lines. In a similar way, the hypocrites valued the approval of the community, so when they had an audience they put on an exaggerated show of piety. When the temple was full of people, the hypocrites tossed their offerings into a metal container so that the large coins clattered against the sides. And when they fasted, they wore a somber face to let everyone know they were practicing self-deprivation.

I'm not innocent myself of putting on a show to win approval. When I still taught aerobics, I attended staff meetings. These meetings were led by our supervisor, and we instructors used the opportunity to let our boss know what a good job we were doing:

"I created some new choreography, and the class just loves it!"; "I've used the same choreography for six weeks and my classes are packed!"; "I just started using negative strength training, and my class members already see improvements in themselves"; "I've been using negative strength training for years and have always had success with it."

Spike, the hypocrites in the Bible, and my colleagues and I are alike in that we all put on a performance in order to gain approval. We are all different, however, in some important ways. Spike is a dog. It is the nature of a dog both to bark at strangers and, since dogs are eager to please, to seek approval. But if someone tried to break into the home of Spike's owners, that scrappy little dog would light into an intruder whether or not the owners were around to show their approval. Dogs are simply territorial at heart.

My colleagues and I might admit to boasting about our classes in order to impress the supervisor. But most of us did our best to give the club members a safe and effective workout, whether or not the boss was watching. We loved our jobs and felt we made a difference in the lives of the members. In other words, our hearts were into it.

The hearts of the hypocrites, however, did not reflect their outward display of piety. In order to gain public approval, they made a show of observing the precepts of the Law, but behaved differently when no one was watching. In private, they cheated people out of money and property and they scorned those who were in need.

Spike's owners are probably not impressed by his showing off, but they know he does his job even when they aren't around. In the case of my colleagues and I, I'm quite certain our boss knew when we were boasting, but she also knew we put our hearts into our jobs, even when the boss wasn't watching. The New Testament community may have been impressed by religious display, but the hypocrites overlooked a couple of things: *their* Boss was always watching, and he knew what was in their hearts—I dare say he wasn't impressed!

There is no greatness where there is not simplicity, goodness and truth.
–Leo Tolstoy

Something is better than nothing.
~Buster and Velvet the dogs

"Is Buster clumsy, or what?" Tom said.

We were taking Velvet and Buster for a walk (what we refer to as a family outing), and the dogs were on leashes in front of us. Occasionally, Buster moved closer to Velvet and bumped against her, then moved away.

"I saw a movie about wolves on public television," I said. "When they hunt in packs, wolves bump against each other for reassurance. The bumping seems to reinforce the bond between pack members. Maybe Buster bumps against Velvet like that as a carry over from their wild ancestors."

Buster, as do all dogs, also needs reassurance from her human pack members. A few words, a touch given now and then during the day—it doesn't take much and something is better than nothing—reassures Buster and Velvet that they are accepted members of the pack. Touching, eye contact, and verbal expression reinforces the bond between me and the two dogs.

When it comes to reinforcing my relationship with God, the something-is-better-than-nothing principal works, too. I've read about people who spend two hours a day in prayer and Bible study. They compile organized prayer lists divided into categories for each day of the week: Monday, pray for the sick; Tuesday, pray for family... And some people set a goal for Bible study—a certain number of chapters a day.

Reading about those people makes me feel pretty inadequate. I thought, *If I can't spend sufficient time in prayer and*

Bible study, I won't be able to have a strong relationship with God. But from my experience with my dogs, I knew that sincere effort—keeping in touch now and then during the day—practiced consistently, could reap meaningful results.

So I started out by reading just one chapter of Scripture every night before going to bed, and then reciting the Lord's prayer. When I drove to my volunteer work, I talked to God instead of to myself: "Help me to be patient with these people and to focus on them instead of on myself."

Over time, reading one chapter of Scripture turned into sometimes reading several chapters; my prayers became more personal: "Forgive me *my* trespasses as I forgive . . ."; "Give me this day my daily bread . . ." Those prayers and Scripture readings, performed consistently, have made an impact on me: I've become more patient, for example, and less self-centered; I'm learning how difficult it sometimes is to forgive, and I'm learning what being forgiving feels like.

Buster and Velvet come next to my chair while I'm writing; Velvet breathes a soft, high whistle and Buster lays her head on my arm. I stop and speak a few words to them, stroke their heads, reassure them and reinforce the bond between us. And in much the same way Buster and Velvet approach me, I go to God at times during the day: "I trust you; lead me; help me to get where I need to go"—when I'm driving, when I'm washing the dishes, when I'm writing.

I send out tiny, thin threads of faith that reinforce the bond between God and me. But though the strands are slender, each alone almost nothing, together they add up to something significant and keep me connected to the Father.

*A dog is a great companion, but I need to have
an open-hearted talk with God.
—Ken Kuykendall*

• GOD'S FAIRNESS •

One bite will get me snacks for life.
–Buster the dog

Early on, my husband made a rule, "No feeding the dogs at the table!" And as long as I'm eating at the table, the dogs ignore me. But one evening I was eating popcorn and watching TV. Without thinking, I tossed a kernel to Buster. This act of incredible lunacy was like opening Pandora's box: Once the lid is off, there's no containing the mischief.

Now if I have a sandwich in front of the TV, I'm surrounded by furry faces that look as if they haven't seen food for a week. Their big moist eyes gaze at my hand as it lifts to my lips, then follow it as it lowers to the plate. Velvet adds an effective touch by drooling onto my shoe.

But then Velvet has the instincts of a thespian. She understands that the silent, wretched stare induces pity in a gullible human. Not so Buster. If I ignore her too long she yelps. I say, "Quiet!" and she swats at me with her paw. I say, "No!" and she yelps.

Some dog trainers say it's okay to give in to your dog as long as you make the dog do something for the treat. So I command Buster, "Down!" She goes into the down position and I throw her a kernel of popcorn. Thirty seconds later she yelps again—from the down position. From then on, I crunch, Buster yelps, I toss. Crunch, yelp, toss, until the bag is empty. Who says rituals have no place in modern culture?

Yes, I'm a wuss. Yes, my dogs are spoiled. Mea culpa. Buster made a little fuss, I gave in. Now she expects a handout every time I eat in front of the TV. Ask and you shall receive.

In the Old Testament, the five daughters of Zelophehad (Num. 27:1-11) must have had similar expectations when they approached Moses with their request. "Our father died in the desert," they said, "and left no sons. Why should [his] name disappear. . . . Give us property among our father's relatives."

Imagine the audacity of these five sisters. At that time in history, women didn't own property. They *were* property. But God had been commanding some pretty revolutionary changes among the Israelites. At a time when cruelty and self-interest prevailed, God laid down rules for the fair treatment of servants and slaves. When sexual promiscuity was the norm, God commanded punishment for adulterers.

God was laying out a whole new way for humankind to relate to each other, and he paid particular attention to the concerns of women. He championed the sanctity of virgins, the rights of widows and orphans, and he assigned value to women and to unborn children. To Zelophehad's daughters, this must have seemed radically pro-female.

Surely, the pattern of God's behavior is what led them to expect he'd honor their request, and is what gave them the courage to stand in front of Moses and the assembled elders of Israel to make that request. Imagine the astonishment that crept over smirking faces when Moses reappeared after consulting with God and announced, "The Lord says, 'You must certainly give them property as an inheritance.'"

Just as my past capitulation to Buster justified her expectations to share in my popcorn, so too did the pattern of God's commands justify the expectations of Zelophehad's daughters in a share of Israel's inheritance.

God is, of course, more gracious and just than I. I still don't share food with my dogs at the table, and they don't even bother to ask. But God tells us we may bring our requests to Him with the expectation of receiving. The five sisters from the Old Testament did, and they didn't have to content themselves with a few kernels of salty popcorn.

Would any of you who are fathers give your son a stone when he asks for bread? You know how to give good things to your children. How much more, then, will your Father in heaven give good things to those who ask him!
–Matthew 7:9–11 (GNB)

Our human is on the phone . . . Let's fight!
~Velvet and Buster the dogs

"I can't hear you," I said. I was on the phone, talking to Mark, a client. "Just a minute." Then with my hand over the receiver, "Velvet, Buster! Quiet!" . . . Back to Mark, . . . "Sorry. My dogs."

My sister called, and Buster put her front paws on my chair, stood on her hind legs, and snuffed into the receiver.

"What?" said Yvonne.

"Sorry. The dog."

I called a mail-order firm, and Velvet paced back and forth to the door, whining as if she couldn't hold it for another second.

"Just a minute!" I hissed at her.

"What?"

"Sorry. My dog."

It never fails. If I'm on the phone for more than a couple of minutes, Velvet and Buster cause a disturbance. Nothing major. They're just trying to get my attention.

God, too, may sometimes use chaos in much the same way. Most people who believe in God assert that he does not cause bad things to happen, but that he may allow a bad thing to happen and then use it for his own purpose.

My mother smoked cigarettes for over fifty years, and as a consequence she developed lung cancer. God did not cause Mother to smoke nor did he cause her lung cancer. But Mother's illness created a crisis for my whole family, and God used that crisis to focus my attention on him.

Before Mother became ill, my faith was weak and I even began to doubt the existence of God. But then I saw my mother face death without fear, in part because of her faith. I felt God at work throughout her illness: in the help we received from friends and from the stranger who called himself Jerry Christmas; in the memories that helped give me the courage to watch my mother die; in the reading matter—a book about heaven and angels—that had been placed into my hands at just the right time; in the very way Mother died—the process was swift and painless.

My mother's premature death was caused by her own unwise decisions, but God did not abandon her. He gave her comfort in illness and showed great mercy in the way she died. God used that crisis to turn my attention toward him. It was the catalyst that precipitated a recommitment to my faith.

When I'm on the phone, Buster and Velvet often cause a minor disturbance. Most of the time I ignore them or make them quiet down. I know they're just trying to get my attention. My life is seldom disrupted by a major crisis, but life does at times become chaotic. And when that happens it's a good idea to take time out and turn to God. He doesn't cause the chaos, but he may use it to let me know that Someone is trying to get my attention.

To see what is in front of one's nose requires a constant struggle.
—George Orwell

When I dig up the garden, I get dirt on my eyebrows.
—Buster the dog

Buster is smart. But she's not good at deductive reasoning.

Not long ago, I discovered holes dug around the hydrangeas. Velvet and Buster were lying on their bellies in the sun, and they both gazed at me—the very picture of innocence. Buster, though, had dirt around her mouth and on her face. Some even clung to those long, coarse hairs that stick out above her eyes.

Buster saw me inspecting the evidence—holes around the hydrangeas—but she didn't know her dirty face would incriminate her. (She didn't even know she had a dirty face.) The jig, as they say, was up.

Unlike dogs, we humans have the capacity to predict what might be the consequences of our actions. I recall an instance, though, when I didn't foresee the outcome of my behavior.

Gossip is sometimes called "dirt," and I'd like to say that gossip has never crossed my lips. That's what I'd like to say. But, like Buster, I've been guilty of digging a little dirt.

When I was a junior in college, I tutored first year students in English composition. I was part of a university-sponsored program in which tutors met once a week with a group of four students. Tutors earned about seven dollars an hour.

Louise, another tutor in the program, told me something about one of our colleagues. "Did you know that Kelly tries to talk her students into taking private tutoring sessions?"

"Private tutoring isn't necessary," I said. "If students are having trouble, they can sign up for additional group tutoring."

"That's right," said Louise. "But private tutors make fifteen dollars an hour! I think Kelly is more interested in money than helping students."

I was shocked—shocked!—that a tutor would be so unscrupulous. I passed on the dirt about Kelly to several people, the last of whom was Madeline, a senior. Madeline also helped train new tutors.

"This is the third time I've heard that story," said Madeline, "and it's not true. I was evaluating Kelly during her tutoring session the day she supposedly promoted herself. One student was having a hard time in all his classes. He has some emotional problems and can't concentrate. Kelly thought he needed more help than she could give him in group tutoring sessions. She suggested he consider getting a private counselor, not a private tutor."

"Oh," I said. I felt embarrassed and ashamed.

Just as Buster couldn't resist digging in the hydrangeas, I hadn't resisted taking a dig at Kelly. I'd spread false stories that put Kelly's integrity at risk. And, like Buster, I was the one who wound up with dirt on my face.

If a man digs a pit, he will fall into it.
–Proverbs 26:27

A little mud never hurt anybody.
–Buster and Velvet the dogs

"Look at Buster!" said my friend Diana. She and I were walking the dogs on a morning in early spring. It had rained the night before, and because there are no sidewalks in the subdivision near my house, we walked in the wet streets. Buster's loose gait flicked up dirt and water, and Velvet went out of her way to walk through puddles. Both dogs were muddy from their paws to their bellies, but the dirt was more visible on Buster's blond fur.

Buster looked up at me and grinned, then bumped against me. "Oh, thank you," I said. "Thank you very much. Now there's a big blob of mud on my pant leg."

"That makes us even," said Diana. "The last time I was here Buster put a dirty paw print on my white sweatshirt."

"Did that spot come out?" I said.

"Oh, sure. Besides, it takes more than a little dirt to come between me and my pals here."

Buster turned her face up to us. Her eyes were as bright as the morning and her tongue dangled from the side of her mouth. Velvet forged ahead and plupped through another puddle. Their opinion was obvious: a little mud never hurt anybody.

Diana had said, "It takes more than a little dirt to come between me and my pals." I feel that way, too. If the dogs get muddy, I dry them off with an old towel then brush out the loose dirt. And if in the process a little mud gets on me, some soap and water takes care of it.

Neither is God afraid of a little mud. No matter how soiled in spirit I may become, I can approach the Father—"Look at me, I'm all dirty. I'm sorry I walked through the mud. Please make me clean"—and he won't push me away. Unlike when I clean up the dogs, though, and some of the mud rubs off on me, God is not vulnerable to dirt. His purity cannot be polluted.

The Bible tells us that God came to us in the person of Jesus. Surely his coming was not a spur-of-the-moment decision. God planned the time and place of his incarnation, he chose the nation into which Jesus would be born, and he selected the ancestors whose blood would course through the veins of Christ. Liars, cheats, a prostitute, a drunkard—all are part of the genealogy of the Savior.

Although many godly people were among the progenitors of Christ, it's instructive that God also selected people whose characters were far from spotless. Surely, then, I can be confident that the spots on my character will not prevent God from listening to my confession, because no spot is able to resist the cleansing of God's forgiveness.

When Velvet and Buster are muddy, they still want to come close to me. They, of course, don't realize they are dirty. They don't even know what dirty means. They just want the reassuring closeness to their pack leader, and they wouldn't understand if I pushed them away. So I clean them as best I can, then I toss my soiled clothing in the machine. It all comes out in the wash.

If my character becomes soiled, however, unlike Velvet and Buster, I am aware of my condition. And unlike my dogs, who are eager to get close to me even when they're muddy, I sometimes hesitate to approach God when my spirit is not in pristine condition. But there is no need to hesitate.

God's holiness is not fragile; his perfection is not diminished when imperfection reaches out to him. When I in sincere regret go to him in prayer, he does not become soiled, but I come away cleaned.

Just as I am and waiting not
to rid my soul of one dark blot.
–Charlotte Elliott

• R I T U A L S •

But I like the same old path.
~Buster and Velvet the dogs

My mom used to say, "If you want your house and yard to look perfect, don't have kids or dogs." Just from looking at our place, it's easy to guess we have dogs. Inside the house, the light-colored rugs are covered with Velvet's black hair, and the dark colored rugs are covered with Buster's blond hair. A rubber bone, a hunk of rope, a fuzzy ball—all in various stages of ruin—lie scattered across the floor. Outside, the fenced-in yard has a couple of shallow craters, some brown spots, and paths worn into the lawn.

The craters are caused from digging, the brown spots are caused by . . . well, not by lack of water . . . and the paths are there because dogs are creatures of habit. When Velvet and Buster go outside, they always take the same route: first, a straight diagonal line from the door to the far corner of the fence, and then a patrol line along the fence.

Buster and Velvet repeat the same behaviors not because they're too lazy or stupid to learn something new. The habits—rituals, if you will—of canines are inherited from their wild ancestors and the rituals have a purpose. First and foremost is to overcome danger: over time, the pack learned that doing certain things and going certain places aided survival. When the learned behaviors were repeated, the pack thrived. Why mess with what works?

I had read that forcing my dogs to deviate from their habits was good for them. It challenged them and stimulated their minds. So I placed a wheelbarrow along their diagonal path. When I let them out they trotted along the path and, without even slowing down, swerved around the wheelbarrow and back onto the path. They knew where they wanted to go, and their little ritual helped them overcome my little obstruction. I put the wheelbarrow back in the garage.

Humans, too, perform rituals. And in ancient times, humans followed certain rituals for much the same reasons that wild canines did: to overcome danger. Making medicines from certain herbs and plants, for instance, required a complex process in order to remove deadly toxins. Committing the steps to memory by following a ritual helped eliminate accidental poisoning.

Because a human being possesses a spiritual as well as a physical nature, human rituals often contain religious elements. And religious rituals help me overcome spiritual obstacles. The Lord's Prayer, for instance, is a ritual prayer. I've known it by heart since childhood, and after I recommitted myself to God, I recited the Lord's Prayer every night: ". . . forgive us our trespasses . . ." As a next step I gave each phrase a personal application: "forgive me my trespasses..." Next, I thought about my actual trespasses—words, deeds, or thoughts that may have offended God or someone I encountered: "forgive me for being rude to the bank clerk; it wasn't his fault the bank instituted another new fee."

Reciting the Lord's Prayer and then personalizing it helped me eventually overcome my uncertainty about talking to God in my own way. But religious rituals do not take the place of living my faith. And they won't get me to heaven. I get to heaven only by confessing that Jesus is God incarnate, that he died to pay for sin—my sin. And that he was resurrected from death.

Placing the wheelbarrow in Velvet and Buster's path did

not keep them from getting where they wanted to go. They merely followed their ritual and the ritual helped them overcome the obstacle. When I pray, my mind sometimes wanders. A self-centered thought might obstruct my concentration. I find that returning to the ritual—reciting the Lord's Prayer—helps me refocus on God.

Rituals are not an end in themselves, neither are they the path to my destination. They can, however, help me overcome obstructions I encounter along the way. And I need all the help I can get to keep me moving straight ahead!

Broad is the road that leads to destruction . . .
narrow the road that leads to life.
–Matthew 7:13-14

If only they could see me now.
~Buster the dog

A mutt is a dog with a unique history. And most of it remains unknown to the family who adopts the mutt. The humane society has a kennel full of unique histories, each one bearing a tale . . . and a tail . . . just waiting for a happy ending.

Buster's tale is a sad one. She was found all by herself on a farm lane. The society staff guessed that she was the last of a litter and was abandoned, left to die of starvation and exposure. At the shelter, we saw a malnourished and dirty little mutt, her eyes glassy, her fur dull and dry. She was full of fleas and intestinal worms—four pounds of sorrowful pup.

At this writing, Buster is a year and a half old and weighs fifty-three pounds. Her fur is thick and luxurious, her eyes are bright, and her face is cheerful and eager. If the people who threw Buster away could see her now, how might they react? Perhaps they breed dogs for profit, so a mutt—no matter how fine looking—has no value to them. Perhaps they'd be unable to believe it's the same dog they rejected. Or they might deny it's the same animal, unable to admit the dog had turned out so well.

Jesus was in the lowest possible condition: he was horribly wounded and dying. Most of his friends had deserted him. By all appearances he was abandoned even by God. In three days' time, though, his appearance changed. Mary Magdalene recognized him as soon as he spoke to her, and she was ready to embrace him. Most of the disciples took a

little convincing, but they soon recognized him as the Lord.
Thomas would not admit to recognizing Jesus until he was
shown proof.

When the disciples—eyewitnesses to the events—related
to others the story of Jesus' life, death, and resurrection,
many listeners believed. Others responded with disinterest
or disbelief.

People who see Buster in her present healthy condition
believe me when I tell about her history, and they believe
even without my stack of photos and documents as support-
ing evidence. The story of Jesus, of his lowly condition on
the cross and his resurrection in a vigorous body, is reinforced by no such concrete proofs as photographs, and the
resurrected Jesus has for two millennia existed in a realm
where we cannot see him.

But if people could see Jesus today, how would they
respond? It so happens Jesus is visible today—in the same
way as he has been for almost two thousand years—through
Scripture, through the personal stories of how Jesus changes
lives, and through the millions who keep the Savior in
their hearts.

People introduced to Jesus through the Bible and through
those who love him respond in the same ways as did his
original disciples. Some recognize him immediately. Others
may not recognize him at first, but then embrace him when
they do recognize who he is. Some may need more persuading than others or may demand convincing proofs, but in the
end they acknowledge that Jesus is Lord. And still others,
despite the evidence, respond with disinterest or disbelief.

But God is patient. And no matter how many times an
unbeliever rejects Jesus, when that person at last recognizes

the Savior and believes in him, God will invite the new believer to take Christ as his or her own. And that's what I call a tale with a happy ending!

Because you have seen me, you have believed; blessed are those who have not seen and yet have believed.
—John 20:29

Rabies and heartworm and fleas, oh my!
~Velvet and Buster the dogs

"Look at them," Tom said. "They have no idea what we do to protect them."

We'd just returned from Velvet's and Buster's annual spring check-ups: physical exams, heartworm testing, rabies booster, a shot for kennel cough and another for DHLPP-CV (whatever that is), and pedicures all around. I held a bag of supplies: heartworm preventative, little vials of stuff that kills fleas, and anti-inflammatory medication (Buster had a minor sprain).

Velvet, good as gold, had sat quietly on the examining table, panting and squinting her way through the ordeal. Buster yelped every time Dr. Leali touched her. When we got home, Velvet and Buster bolted out of the car, scrabbled across the cement walk, and streaked out into the yard, where they both . . . paused.

By the time Tom and I gathered up veterinary receipts and supplies and had closed up the garage, Velvet and Buster were playing tag. They streaked across the yard nose to tail, with Velvet in the lead, and then they leaned into a 180 degree turn, which put Buster in the lead. This maneuver was repeated a couple of times until they had burned off some nervous energy. Then they headed for the door and, once inside the house, straight for the water dish.

Our healthy, happy dogs have no clue how much money and effort is spent to protect them from attack by various pests and ailments. They don't even know that they are under attack!

I wonder if I'm aware of all that menaces me. When I pray "give me this day my daily bread," I interpret that as "thank you for my daily bread." I express gratitude, as well, for less humidity today than yesterday, electric fans in the summer, flannel sheets in the winter—and for close calls that easily could have gone bad.

A close call is not only something like a narrow miss while driving the car; a close call may be spiritual in nature. With God's help, I've dealt with overt spiritual attacks—skirmishes with vanity, hopelessness, pride, greed, envy. But in the book of Luke, Jesus says to Peter: "Satan has asked to sift you as wheat. But I have prayed for you [Peter] that your faith may not fail" (22:31-32). Has Satan asked to sift me, to launch an attack against which Jesus has interceded on my behalf? The Bible also says we will never be tempted beyond that which we are able to resist (1 Cor. 10:13). So how many temptations has Christ, knowing my weaknesses, prevented from being placed in my path?

Velvet and Buster are unaware of the pests and parasites that can attack their health. Neither are they aware of the energy and expense that go into keeping them robust and healthy. But they do, I think, know when they are not having a good time and when they are having a good time. A visit to the veterinarian is not having a good time. Playing tag on a sunny spring morning is without question having a good time.

Unlike Velvet and Buster, I'm aware that I am vulnerable—that my soul is under constant spiritual attack. Resisting temptations is not what I'd call having a good time, but I know that the confrontation makes me stronger for the next temptation. And if Jesus' statement to Peter is any indication, I am probably unaware of the actual number of hurdles that were removed before I ever got to them. So, for Jesus' intercession until I can build up more spiritual muscle—thank you, Father.

And if my dogs' game of tag is how they show gratitude for my intercession on their behalf—you're welcome, Velvet and Buster.

In this world you will have trouble. But take heart!
I have overcome the world.
-John 16:33

Real dogs don't say "cheese."
—Jet the dog

Look! I found these old snapshots of Jet. In this one he's just a puppy—about ten weeks old—and he's racing around the yard with a stuffed elephant in his mouth (he always preferred soft toys to hard ones).

Here's one when he was about five months old; I don't know why he's staring at that bucket of water, but in this next one—see—he's biting at the water from the garden hose. I guess playing with running water is more fun than drinking it out of a pail.

He's full-grown in this one, and I caught him eating the petals off those purple tulips.

These images were not captured by a professional photographer. Jet is not fresh from the groomer wearing a red bow, nor is he arranged in a pose of idealized canine cuteness. I took these pictures with an old instamatic camera. That's why the quality isn't very good—the images are tilted and off center; a couple of them are blurred; the lighting is poor. But these few snapshots are precious to me because Jet has been dead for many years and these are the only pictures of him that I have.

And they capture something—don't you think?—a little of his spirit, his personality. And only a little, because a picture conveys only an idea of the real Jet and what he really looked like. You can see his blond fur, for instance, but you can't see how the beiges blended in with the almost-whites. You can see his dark eyes, but you can't see how big and bright they got on cold days, or how deep and utterly content when he lay by the fire.

These images don't tell the whole story of Jet, any more than the Bible tells the whole story of God. But the Bible holds the closest thing we have to pictures of God, with snapshots of him mounted on every page. No individual photograph conveys a complete portrait of God; none of them reveal his face. But taken together, the images convey an idea of what God is like—his nature and character—by what he's doing in the pictures.

Genesis shows God's creative nature. Exodus is like a double exposure—compassion and anger in the countenance of God the Father. He rescues and nourishes his children, the Israelites. At the same time he disciplines them. In Psalms, the pictures reflect God's love for music and poetry. Throughout the Prophets the images reveal God's long-suffering as he warns his erring children again and again of their coming destruction.

The pictures of God in the New Testament come into much sharper focus because God's nature is imaged in a man called Jesus. These snapshots show Jesus healing people and feeding large crowds, and—among my favorites—Jesus holding a child, having intimate conversation with an outcast woman, and writing in the dust near the feet of a sinful woman.

The pictures of God in the Bible share two characteristics with my pictures of Jet: First, they do not give a clear and complete image. But I can tell stories about Jet and describe him in such detail that one could imagine him quite well. The complete nature of our infinite God, on the other hand, is beyond finite human imagination.

Second, the two sets of pictures are candid and unsentimental. Jet is not puffed and pedicured or placed in an idealized pose. Neither do the Old Testament images of God glamorize his nature or focus on just the deity we're comfortable hearing about. Though they show him as merciful, compassionate, and nurturing, they also show him angry and administering severe justice. In the Gospels, God seems less fearsome, but he is not dressed up as the King of the universe. He does not pose in a robe of state or jeweled crown. Instead he emerges as a common laborer dressed in a robe of rough and plain material.

My shaggy little white dog has long been dead, and I treasure these few concrete images, not in spite of but because of their unprofessional quality. I value the pictures of God in the Bible for much the same reason. They were produced through ordinary men—not professional myth makers—who were commissioned by God to create honest images. I suppose a puffed and powdered, sentimental portrait of God would be a lot easier for some people to accept. But I prefer to see those I love as they really are, not shot through a sepia-colored lens to artificially soften the image.

The real Jet didn't pose for the camera and say cheese. The real Jet was sometimes sweet and sometimes naughty, and that's how I want to remember him. The real God is love and compassion, but he is also anger and justice that is not sepia-soft around the edges. And the real God will not pose in front of a filtered lens and smile for the camera.

I will behold thy face in righteousness: I shall be satisfied.
~Psalm 17:15 (KJV)

Do F look like Western Union?
~Velvet and Buster the dogs

I could take a clue from my dogs; they don't obsess. They don't fix their minds on some object or activity and give it unwarranted priority in their lives. They might vie for possession of the bone-on-a-rope, but thirty seconds later they forget the toy and nap together on the couch. If Tom takes Velvet for a walk, Buster doesn't nurse a grudge. If I refuse Velvet a bite of my chocolate donut the whole matter is forgotten when the last crumb disappears.

When Buster gets tired, she doesn't fret, *I can't go to bed until I finish cleaning my paws!* When Velvet wants to chase a chipmunk she doesn't think, *No! I first have to finish chewing on this stick.*

It's not possible, of course, to live like Velvet and Buster and do whatever strikes my fancy whenever I feel like it. But neither is it healthy to do the opposite, to become so obsessed with something—like personal appearance or work—that life revolves around the obsession.

One of my former colleagues, an aerobics instructor named Bev, obsessed on diet and exercise. Sensible eating and regular exercise hold an important place in a balanced life, but Bev seems to think of little else. I happened to see her at a shoe store awhile ago.

"How was your weekend?" I said.

"Oh . . . my husband's parents were visiting and my mother-in-law got mad at me because I wouldn't eat a piece of the cheesecake she brought," Bev said.

"I heard the instructors gave Nancy a baby shower. Did you go?"

"No, I couldn't. I had a walk-a-thon for a charity and I thought I'd better do it because I needed to lose two pounds. Nice to see you! Gotta go! I have to do my four-mile jog before the kids get home from school."

" . . . Bye."

I have no business pointing a finger at Bev, though. It's easy for me to become obsessed about work—to fret when I don't have a project or to work nonstop on a project even when it isn't due for two weeks.

Readers might think that I obsess on my dogs; here's a whole book dedicated to observing their behavior. But—honest—I do not follow Velvet and Buster all day, waiting for the next spiritual message as if my dogs served as Western Union for God. Watching dogs is fun, though, and in the next life perhaps I'll be able to spend a couple of thousand years doing just that.

In the meantime my life needs balance: I need to work and I need to rest, I need nourishing food . . . and sometimes I need a chocolate donut. I need exercise to offset the chocolate donut. I need entertainment . . . and I need to serve; I need solitude and I need companionship. I need to pray and read the Bible.

I find myself more and more considering things of the soul, keeping in touch with God, asking where he's leading. I keep a small ceramic angel in the car, and a crystal angel— a gift from my husband—sits on the windowsill by the computer. My Bible lies on the bureau next to the bed, and a tiny cross hangs in the window above the kitchen sink. These are only objects—not objects of worship—and they serve a function: When I see them I'm reminded of the presence of God.

I suppose it's possible to become overly preoccupied about even spiritual concerns; if I directed every conversation to God, the Bible, the soul, the afterlife; if that's *all* I ever talked about, people might start avoiding me. Still, while I'm working and resting and exercising and, yes, watching my dogs, I can keep the lines of communication open between God and me. He may have a message for me and deliver it at a most unlikely time or place.

Oh, look! Velvet and Buster are—

Never mind. I wouldn't want you to think I'm obsessed.

The trail is the thing, not just the end of the trail.
Travel too fast and you miss all you are traveling for.
—Louis L'Amour

I am here for but a season . . .
~Canis familiaris

"I'm really going to miss being at home," Tom said.

Velvet, Buster, and I stood at the gate while Tom put his gear in the car. He was leaving for a training seminar, and he walked back to me for a good-bye kiss.

"I'll miss you, too, dear," I said and got ready to pucker up.

Instead, he bent down and ruffled an ear on each dog. "Yeah," he said. "I didn't know that having two dogs was going to be so much fun!"

I don't blame Tom for missing the dogs. Before he and I married, and he acquired Jet as part of the deal, my husband hadn't had a dog of his own since he was four years old. As a little boy, he surely felt his pet—the first Buster—was gone too soon. Then Jet had a stroke when Tom was out of town, and before he got home, the little dog was gone.

When Velvet was about four years old we talked about getting another puppy, then suddenly Velvet was six. She and Tom were cuddled on the couch one evening, and when I looked at them my face likely bore an expression similar to that of a doting mother.

"You're sure going to miss her when she's gone," I said.

Within two weeks we had Buster.

I sometimes refer to our group as a family, and I've heard people say, "My dog thinks she's a person." Mike, the trainer, says, "There's no dog alive that thinks he's a person. More likely a dog thinks a human is a very superior dog." So

Velvet and Buster likely look at our group as a pack, and they have no idea that the pack will not go on forever.

A dog's life span is brief. They are gone too soon and that makes me sad. Having several dogs in my lifetime, though, gives me the opportunity to atone for the mistakes I make with them. When Jet was a young dog he wasn't neutered, didn't have a safe place to exercise and play, and had no pack members to interact with. I rectified those mistakes as Jet got older, and now Velvet and Buster benefit from my more responsible approach to dog ownership. And what I've learned about obedience training and discipline with Velvet and Buster will benefit our next dog.

Humans live much longer than dogs, but we are still gone too soon. My mother was seventy-three years old when she died. Some people might say seventy-three is a good life span, but I was not ready to lose her. I'm not ready to lose anyone I love, and I have no opportunity—at least not in the same way as with dogs—to rectify the mistakes I make with the people I care about. I won't get a chance, for instance, to be a better child with my next mother or spend more time with my next sister. Nor do I even want to contemplate having a "next husband" or "next best friend" with whom to be more patient or considerate. No, with people I get very few second chances. Parents, siblings, husband, friends . . . and I . . . I, too, will be gone too soon.

God's love and mercy, however, endure forever, and the Father has provided me with free will. I can change my behavior. My parents are dead, so although I cannot be a better daughter, I can do volunteer work with seniors. I can be more patient with my husband, make more time for my sister, act more considerately toward my friends. I cannot start all over with loved ones in the same way I have done with my dogs, but I can learn from the past mistakes I've made with people and build a better present.

My heart swells when I consider all that the Father has provided: He gave me life and provided for my eternal life. He encourages an intimate walk with him and gives me the opportunity to create intimacy with family and friends. Then as an act of extraordinary generosity, he gave me the love and friendship of creatures like Velvet and Buster who have canine instincts: an affectionate disposition, the need to bond with the pack leader, a nature that responds to discipline, praise, and kindness. That makes them fit right into my household.

I cannot help but praise Him.

*Put [your] hope in God, who richly provides us
with everything for our enjoyment.
–1 Timothy 6:17*

Augustine believed that all of creation is an expression of God's thoughts and feelings. On this warm and muggy June evening a storm sweeps through, and I am awash in a host of thoughts and feelings.

The lightning and thunder, the force of the wind demonstrate the power of the Creator—*how great thou art.*

Velvet is hiding in the bathtub. The boom and crack of the storm alarm her, and she feels safer in the dark and quiet of the bathroom. Her behavior reminds me that it is prudent to regard God's might with awe and wonder. And though I, like Velvet, sometimes feel dread or anxiety, I also have a place I can retreat to—*God* is my refuge.

Buster, however, stands next to me on the porch. She wags her tail and grins at me, totally untroubled by the rumble and flash of the storm. Her comical expression provided a balance to my sober regard for God's might. Buster reminds me that there is room for humor in faith—there is a time to laugh.

God created both a tempest and a wagging tail—one expresses power, the other expresses love. And while God is worthy of respect for his power, he is also worthy of devotion because of his love.

After the storm, a fresh breeze lifts the curtain at the bedroom window. Three striped scatter rugs—one on either side of the bed and one at the foot—decorate the hardwood floor.

Velvet has come in and lies sprawled in the exact center of one rug. Buster is curled up on another.

I look from Buster to Velvet, and my gaze stops at the empty rug. "Honey," I say to Tom, "look at this poor lonesome rug. Don't you think we need another dog?"

SHARE THE GIFT OF

$\mathcal{C}$anine
$\mathcal{P}$arables

Portraits of God and Life

ORDER ADDITIONAL COPIES FOR
FRIENDS & DOG LOVERS
IN YOUR LIFE

GREAT BOOKS TO ENRICH YOUR LIFE!

What the Church Owes the Jew
~Leslie B. Flynn

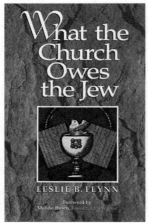

What do you know about the unique Jewish contribution to the Scriptures, the Church, and to the world at-large?
Dr. Leslie Flynn, who served as pastor to many Jewish Christians in the New York area, passionately shares these answers and more (e.g., anti-Semitism, the Jewishness of Jesus), to help Jews and non-Jews build bridges of understanding and friendship.
ISBN 0-9654806-3-1 paper $12.00

Positive Attitudes for the 50+ Years:
How Anyone Can Make Them Happy & Fulfilling
~Willard A. Scofield

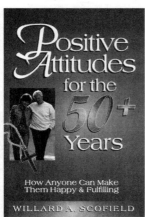

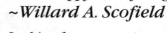

Looking for answers to some of the uncertainties of the 50+ Years?
Willard Scofield, former associate editor for *Decision* magazine, and a Peale Center Guidance Counselor, shares insights to 75 often asked questions. Whether you have spiritual, financial, personal, relational, or other questions, you will find the answers in this helpful, biblically-based handbook.
ISBN 0-9654806-2-3 paper $12.00

Yes We Can Love One Another!
Catholics and Protestants Can Share A Common Faith
~*Warren Angel*

You've heard and read a lot about the things Catholics and Protestants don't have in common!

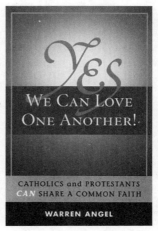

Here's a book which tells you what we *do* have in common. You don't have to change churches to learn how to love other believers in Jesus Christ. Warren Angel helps remove barriers to fellowship by breaking down misconceptions Christians believe about each other, and shows us how, in Christ, we can be a Church of power and joy in the Holy Spirit.
ISBN 0-9654806-0-7 paper $12.00

Jesus in the Image of God: *A Challenge to Christlikeness*
~*Leslie B. Flynn*

A great book for Bible study groups!

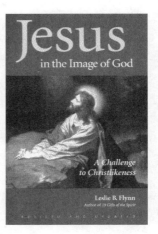

Here's a real antidote to the negative and faithless views of the Jesus Seminar. Let the Jesus of the Gospels challenge you to become more like him—the Son of God created in God's own image, who overcame despair, sorrow, rejection, and humiliation to bring healing, redemption, hope, and the Good News of God's love to all human beings.
ISBN 0-9654806-1-5 paper $12.00

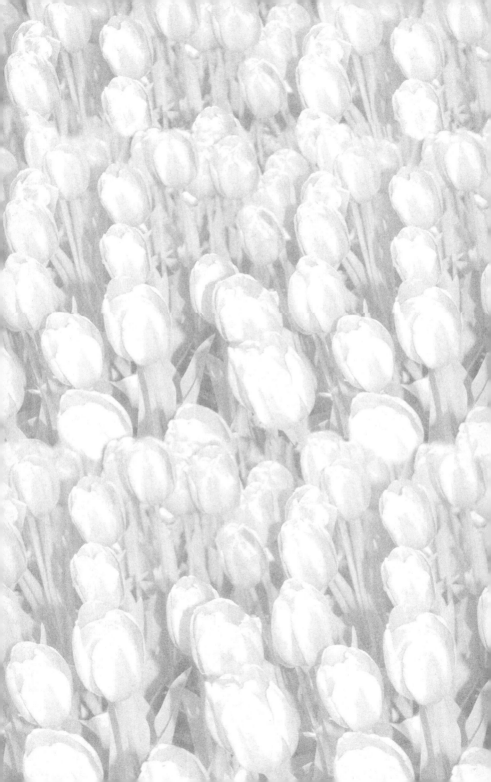